WEIRD AND WILD VANCOUVER

Harrison Mooney

BLUE
BIKE
BOOKS

First printed in 2012 10 9 8 7 6 5 4 3 2 1

Printed in Canada

The Publisher: Blue Bike Books

Website: www.bluebikebooks.com

Library and Archives Canada Cataloguing in Publication

Mooney, Harrison

    Weird and wild Vancouver / Harrison Mooney.

ISBN 978-1-926700-11-3

    1. Vancouver (B.C.)—Miscellanea. I. Title.

FC3847.3.M66 2012   971.1'33   C2012-900325-5

Project Director: Nicholle Carrière
Project Editor: Kathy van Denderen
Cover Image: Upside-down church and foreground - ©2012 Keith Levit / Design Pics; Vancouver skyline - ©2000–2009 ©Chrisarchytekt | Dreamstime.com; sky - Photos.com
Illustrations: Pat Bidwell, Roger Garcia, Patrick Hénaff, Djordje Todorovic, Peter Tyler, Roly Wood

Produced with the assistance of the Government of Alberta, **Government of Alberta** ■
Alberta Multimedia Development Fund

We acknowledge the financial support of the Government of Canada through the Canada Book Fund (CBF) for our publishing activities.

 Canadian Patrimoine
Heritage canadien

PC: 1

For Christy

CONTENTS

ACKNOWLEDGEMENTS

This book is dedicated to my wife, Christy, who allowed me to lock myself in a room for months on end working on it while paying no attention to her, the cat, the state of our house, the bills, current events, the time of day or even my own personal hygiene or health. She brought me food, she vacuumed the crumbs from under my feet, she waited until she was downstairs (where she thought I couldn't hear her) to sigh at my obsessiveness and she encouraged the bejesus out of me. It is not possible to find a woman more perfectly suited to a problem husband like me, and I want her to know that she is loved and valued more than anything else in my life.

While I'm at it, thanks to Greg, Daniel and Sean for being patient and accommodating; Mom, Dad, Max, Ben and Sam for being my family (I think you guys are swell); Bill, Linda, Mike, Pablo, Erika, Brenda, Emma and Isabel for being my other family (I also think you guys are swell); Andrew Fleming for getting me started; and Zora for reminding me that there are more important things in life than getting one's work done, especially when the outdoors await. And finally, thanks to the staff at Blue Bike Books and Kathy for their open-mindedness, kindness and patience.

City Timeline

Without question it may be said of Vancouver that her position, geographically, is Imperial to a degree, that her possibilities are enormous, and that with but a feeble stretch of the imagination those possibilities might wisely be deemed certainties.

–A.N. Homer, historian

A BRIEF HISTORY OF VANCOUVER

1791: José María Narváez, a Spanish naval officer, leads the exploration of the Strait of Georgia and becomes the first European to enter Burrard Inlet.

1792: Captain George Vancouver, the explorer for whom the city is named, commands an expedition charged with exploring the Pacific region. He enters Burrard Inlet on June 13, naming it after his friend Sir Harry Burrard. George briefly mistakes the area, later named Stanley Park, for an island. While exploring the Point Grey region, he comes across a Spanish expedition and is mortified to learn that they already have a crude chart of the Strait of Georgia, because of Narváez's explorations from the year earlier.

1808: Simon Fraser, a fur trader and explorer, becomes the first European to reach the area by land, descending the river that is later named for him. The permanent settlements he establishes in the area will go a long way toward creating the Canadian boundary at the 49th parallel.

1818: The USA and the United Kingdom sign the Treaty of 1818, also known as the London Convention, which resolves a number of boundary issues between the two nations and provides for joint control of the land in the Oregon Country. While the agreement is relatively friendly and involves a great deal of proposed sharing, it only serves to ignite a bitter struggle for control of the Oregon Country over the following two decades. By the 1830s, the Hudson's Bay Company tries to exterminate all fur-bearing animals in the area, just to discourage American settlement.

1846: The Treaty of Washington permanently establishes the 49th parallel as the boundary between the United States and British North America to the Pacific Ocean, meaning everyone will stop wastefully killing beavers out of spite.

1858: Gold is discovered on the Thompson River, not far from its confluence with the Fraser River, kicking off the Fraser Canyon Gold Rush. Over the next year, 30,000 prospectors make their way into the northwest region in search of gold.

1858: The colony of British Columbia is established.

1859: New Westminster is named as the colony's capital.

1866: The Colony of British Columbia and the Colony of Vancouver Island are united as British Columbia, with the capital at Victoria.

1867: Hastings Mill, a sawmill on the south shore of Burrard Inlet and the first commercial operation around which the settlement of Vancouver will develop, is founded.

1867: John "Gassy Jack" Deighton opens the Globe Saloon. The community that builds up around this popular bar becomes known as Gastown, although it is officially surveyed as Granville Townsite only two years later.

1867: Weekly stage service is established between the Brighton Hotel, a popular summer vacation spot just west of the Second Narrows Bridge, and New Westminster.

1883: The first locomotive arrives in Vancouver...on a ship. It's used primarily for local work.

1885: The last spike of the CPR is driven at Craigellachie, on November 7. Although the railway would not open for another six months, this symbolic moment in the nation's history marked the end of a saga of natural and financial disasters that plagued the railway's development from day one.

1886: To the surprise of many (and because of some promises of free land), the CPR selects Granville as the western terminus for its grand continental line, immediately making the small community of 1000 the prominent settlement on Canada's west coast. With the announcement comes a massive boom in population and development. The city is incorporated as the City of Vancouver, the name chosen by the CPR president William Van Horne. Citizens elect Malcolm Alexander MacLean, a real estate dealer, as the first mayor of Vancouver.

1886: Vancouver General Hospital opens on Pender Street. The Vancouver Rowing Club is formed.

1886: The Vancouver Police Department is formed. The first badges are made of American silver dollars, with one side smoothed down and engraved "Vancouver City Police."

1886: The Great Vancouver Fire breaks out on June 13, razing all but five or six of Vancouver's buildings. Among the surviving structures is the Hastings Mill Store, which is used as a hospital and morgue for the fire victims.

1887: The CPR completes the extension of its westward line to Vancouver. Engine 374 brings the first transcontinental train into Vancouver on May 23.

1887: The SS *Abyssinia*, a British mail ocean liner, opens a new Pacific service. It takes only 13 days to reach Vancouver from Yokohama, Japan, a new trans-Pacific record. The ship's freight of silk and tea is transferred by rail to New York via Montréal only eight days later, and loaded onto another ship that arrives in London another eight days after that. Vancouver thus becomes a major world port.

1888: Stanley Park, Vancouver's world-famous 1001-acre oceanside park, opens.

1888: The first real estate board in Canada is formed in Vancouver.

1888: The *Vancouver Daily World* is founded—the city's first newspaper.

1889: The original Granville Street Bridge, the first of many bridges built to span the False Creek Inlet, is completed.

1897: The Klondike Gold Rush boosts a continent-wide depression of the 1890s, sending thousands of hopeful prospectors to the Pacific coast. By 1900, Vancouver displaces Victoria, the provincial capital, as the leading commercial centre on Canada's west coast.

1898: The Nine O'Clock Gun, a cannon used to alert fishermen of the time, is placed at Brockton Point.

1903: The Woodward's building, which will serve as Vancouver's major shopping destination for much of the 20th century, is constructed.

1907: Two years after the Asiatic Exclusion League (AEL) is formed in San Francisco, a sister group is created in Vancouver. The AEL is a racist organization aimed at preventing the immigration of people of East Asian origin and, suffice it to say, just causes problems. A month after AEL's establishment, a riot breaks out in Chinatown when thousands descend on the community after hearing AEL speeches at City Hall.

1909: The Dominion Trust Building, Vancouver's first skyscraper, is built at Hastings and Cambie. At the time of its completion, the 13-storey structure was the tallest commercial building in the British Empire.

1910: The first Pacific National Exhibition is held in Hastings Park.

1911: The Denman Arena, an artificial ice rink, opens to the public. It soon becomes the home of the Pacific Coast Hockey Association's Vancouver Millionaires, who boast the distinction of being the only Vancouver hockey team to win the Stanley Cup. They did it in 1915.

1914: The *Komagata Maru* incident saw 376 East Asian passengers aboard a Japanese steamship of the same name refused entry into Canada and forced to return to India because of Canada's anti-immigration laws.

1915: Seven years after BC legislation established the University of British Columbia, the first day of lectures takes place when UBC opens its Fairview district campus on September 30.

1918: The Vancouver general strike, the first of its kind in Canadian history, is held on August 2. The one-day protest was against the killing of draft dodger Albert Goodwin, who called for a protest if any worker was drafted against his will. Unsurprisingly, the protest turns unruly, and 300 men storm the Vancouver Trades and Labour Council office and try to throw its secretary, Victor Midgely, out a window.

1923: The Shipping Federation breaks a strike of Vancouver's waterfront workers trying to organize with the International Longshoreman's Association (ILA) by lining up 350 men with shotguns along the pier. The ILA was defeated, and the Shipping Federation establishes the Vancouver and District Waterfront Workers' Association, a company union, in its place.

1925: The original Second Narrows Bridge, the first bridge across Burrard Inlet, connects the municipalities of Vancouver and North Vancouver. After a number of ships collide with the bridge, a lift section is added to the deck in 1933.

1925: The University of British Columbia (UBC) moves from Fairview to its permanent home in Point Grey.

1926: The Orpheum Theatre opens to the public.

1927: Vancouver is shunned by aviator Charles Lindbergh, who refuses to include the city in his North American tour because it lacks a proper airport. Two years later, the city purchases the land on Sea Island that will become the Vancouver International Airport.

1929: Vancouver amalgamates with the municipalities of Point Grey and South Vancouver.

1934: Malkin Bowl, an outdoor theatre built as a two-thirds-size replica of the Hollywood Bowl, presents the first performance of the Vancouver Symphony Orchestra.

1935: Unhappy with the direction the Vancouver and District Waterfront Workers' association has gone, especially after the supposed "company union" elects militant members of the Communist Party of Canada to be its executives, the Shipping Federation incites another strike, hoping once again to break the union. The waterfront workers aren't as easily intimidated this time, and a violent battle ensues on Ballantyne Pier between marchers and armed police. The dispute becomes more demure after that, but it succeeds when the waterfront workers finally get their independent union in 1937.

1936: The new Vancouver City Hall at 12th and Cambie is completed.

1937: The Non-Partisan Association (NPA), perhaps the most ironically named political organization ever, is formed. The centre-right party is founded to counteract the rise of the left-leaning Co-operative Commonwealth Federation. There have been 11 NPA mayors of Vancouver, the most recent being Sam Sullivan, whose term ended in 2008.

1938: The RCMP forcibly evict members of the Relief Camp Workers Union, a group protesting unemployment, after a month-long occupation of Vancouver's main post office.

The interaction escalates into violence on Sunday, June 19, with 42 men hospitalized, five of them police constables. The incident, dubbed "Bloody Sunday," sparks criticisms of police brutality.

1938: The Lions' Gate Bridge, officially known as the First Narrows Bridge for its placement across the first narrowing of Burrard Inlet, opens.

1939: The Fairmont Hotel, originally the Hotel Vancouver—the third building in the city to receive the name—is completed.

1942: Vancouver Magic Circle, one of the world's largest rings of the International Brotherhood of Magicians, is formed.

1953: Vancouver's first TV station, CBUT, launches on December 16, broadcasting from a converted auto dealership in downtown Vancouver. It remains the flagship CBC TV station for the Pacific Time Zone.

1954: Construction on Empire Stadium is completed. The British Empire and Commonwealth Games are held there July 30 to August 7. One of the greatest races in track and field history, "The Miracle Mile," is run on the final day of the Games.

1956: Thanks to generous grants of $100,000 from three levels of government—the City of Vancouver, the Province of British Columbia and the federal government—as well as donations by businessmen H.R. MacMillan and George Cunningham, the Vancouver Aquarium opens in Stanley Park. It is and will always be awesome.

1958: Vancouver Opera, the largest opera in Western Canada, is founded.

1960: The Ironworkers Memorial Second Narrows Crossing opens.

1963: The BC Lions lose the Grey Cup at home, falling 21–10 to the Hamilton Tiger-Cats. A riot breaks out, one of several Vancouver riots with embarrassing motivations.

1964: Led by the great Joe Kapp, the BC Lions win the Grey Cup for the first time in their 10-year history.

1970: The Vancouver Canucks play their first game in the NHL at the Pacific Coliseum. They lose, which will be a common theme for years to come.

1971: The Gastown Riot, also known as the Battle of Maple Tree Square, occurs on August 7. The conflict occurs after 2000 protesters take part in a peaceful "Smoke-in" in favour of legalizing marijuana. The scene becomes heated (no pun intended), with officers handing out indiscriminate beatings and arresting 79 people.

1971: The provincial government designates Gastown and Chinatown as historic districts, and the 10-kilometre pedestrian seawall at Stanley Park officially opens. The designation of all three sites gives Vancouver much of its distinctive flavour.

1982: The Vancouver International Film Festival, which showcases both Canadian and international films, is held for the first time. Today, over 150,000 attend the festival annually, making it one of the five largest film festivals in North America.

1982: The Vancouver Canucks make it to the Stanley Cup final for the first time. They lose. This will become a trend.

1985: A year before Expo '86, SkyTrain opens. The mass transit system runs mostly on elevated guideways and has a significant impact on the development of the surrounding areas, with a 37 percent increase in the population near stations. Four years later, construction on the SkyBridge, a cable-supported bridge that crosses the Fraser River and allows the SkyTrain to go from New Westminster to Surrey, is completed. It is the longest bridge of its kind in the world.

1986: Vancouver celebrates its centennial by hosting Expo '86 on the north shore of False Creek. Charles and Diana, the Prince and Princess of Wales, open the fair on Friday, May 2.

1994: The Vancouver Canucks reach the Stanley Cup finals for the second time in 12 years. They even win some games this time, but in the end, they fall in seven games to the New York Rangers. Fans riot in the streets of downtown Vancouver following the loss.

1995: The city gets two more major structures, as the new Vancouver Public Library, built in the shape of a Roman coliseum, opens on May 26. Only two months later, General Motors Place, a new hockey, basketball and entertainment complex designed to hold both the Vancouver Canucks and the Vancouver Grizzlies basketball team, opens.

2003: Translink U-Pass is implemented. The U-Pass system allows Vancouver students unlimited travel in all zones on buses, the SkyTrain and the SeaBus.

2006: A series of rainstorms in November cause landslides into Vancouver's three main reservoirs, contaminating the drinking water far beyond the legal safety limit and forcing the issuance of boil water advisories for all two million residents. It is the largest such advisory in Canadian history.

2007: A Polish immigrant named Robert Dziekański arrives at the Vancouver International Airport, only to find himself held up at Customs and eventually missing his mother, who had come to pick him up. After nearly a full day stranded at the airport and unable to find anyone who speaks his language, Dziekański becomes agitated.

Four RCMP officers try to calm him down, but tensions rise and the man is tasered multiple times. The act causes Dziekański's heart to stop, killing him. The incident raises debate about the use of tasers in Canada.

2010: The Winter Olympics are held in Vancouver and Whistler. The Canadian athletes put in the best showing in Canadian Olympic history, bringing home a whopping 26 medals, 14 of them gold.

2011: The Vancouver Canucks hockey team reach the Stanley Cup finals for the third time in 40 years, only to lose out to the Boston Bruins. Once again, fans riot in the streets of downtown Vancouver because, at this point, it's become a tradition.

INTRODUCTION

It has been said that Vancouver is an accidental city, and as I was writing this book, I finally got it. Were it not for the decision of the Canadian Pacific Railway (CPR) to establish its Western terminus in Vancouver, perhaps this city would be no larger than, say, Chilliwack. And were the CPR not bribed with so much land, perhaps they wouldn't have hired a brilliant mind like Lauchlan Hamilton to map the city in which they suddenly owned property and plan a fiscally lucrative development.

One wonders what would have come of the city had the border between Canada and the United States been established, say, above Vancouver rather than neatly below it. And what this city might be if Gassy Jack hadn't waddled into town promising free booze to everyone who helped him build a bar on land he didn't own, or worse, if someone had pointed out you're not allowed to do that.

Much of Vancouver's beauty is accidental. Not the dazzling mountainsides iced like a wedding cake or the shimmering ocean or the greenery that seems to be everywhere you turn or the fabulously mild weather—those wonders are no accident.

But what if Stanley Park hadn't been set aside as a ploy to increase the property value of the land around it? What if the Great Fire hadn't inspired the emphasis on brickwork that gives the downtown core so much of its old-world charm? What if L.D. Taylor hadn't been shamed into building the Vancouver Airport with a Charles Lindbergh gut-punch and a propeller to the head?

And what of the people? These pages are filled with influential thinkers who wandered into town looking for something to do, or came up from the south looking for a fresh start. What if they landed somewhere else? They could just as easily have.

Vancouver may not be a total accident, but the city certainly didn't develop as planned.

Thank God for that. A quick read through these pages will give you a thorough idea of the lunatics, madmen and wackos who inhabited this town, and the weird and wild way in which it grew. How many times has the Hudson's Bay Company had to replace its windows? Seventeen? How many post-championship-loss riots can one city have? We're sitting at three and a half right now. How many times can the whites try to run the Chinese out of town? Wisdom is a rarity in these pages.

Judging from the people who led Vancouver into the 20th century, it seems to me that had the settlement not unexpectedly succeeded, it would have deservedly failed. But it didn't, and it thrills me to share with you the great many oddities of British Columbia's accidental metropolis.

Takin' It to the Streets

*I'd rather walk than drive a car. In Vancouver,
where I am from, you can get to just about anywhere
you need to go on foot. Even if it's raining I'll go out
for a stroll. I just love that.*

–Kristin Kreuk, actress

NAME THAT STREET

Vancouver is one of the few major cities in North America without a freeway into the downtown core. Driving can be a hassle at times, especially when the traffic is heavy, which is pretty much all the time.

The moment you take one of the highway off-ramps into the downtown core, you have no choice but to resign yourself to plenty of waiting, looking up at red lights and green street signs for the foreseeable future.

But the situation is not completely bad. One of the joys of Vancouver's lack of shortcuts is that there's no shortage of great streets. Any trip across town is guaranteed to send you through a handful of roads with a story to tell.

Wonder why Pender Street curves for no reason whatsoever? There's a story behind that. Wonder why all the east-west streets are named after trees that seem to have been drawn from a hat? There's a story, too. And if you happen to find yourself on Midlothian Avenue, well, think of William B. Young, the man who loved one writer so much he somehow managed to sprinkle references to the author's body of work all over the city of Vancouver.

Nearly every street in Vancouver tells a story, and often it's all about what's in the name.

Hamilton Street, and Other Streets Named by Lauchlan Hamilton

Lauchlan Hamilton, a land commissioner and the official surveyor for the Canadian Pacific Railway (CPR), was only a Vancouverite from 1885 to 1887, but he's responsible for much of the city's downtown structure, not to mention the names of many of its streets. As the CPR prepared to install its Western terminus in Vancouver, Hamilton was sent ahead from out East to help establish a development plan for the area, which was sure to see a population boom. He sat on the community's first municipal council and drew up his remarkably detailed plans for the city's downtown core, well beyond the spatial needs of the time.

It was difficult and arduous work, as Hamilton had to envision what a densely forested area would look like settled. With so much to do in so little time, Hamilton didn't take much time naming the streets. Many were given the names of CPR employees, some were taken from an admiralty chart of the Pacific Coast and many others were named after prominent men in the British government. In effect, if a name came to mind during Hamilton's brainstorming sessions, it wound up on a street sign.

Mis-tree-ted

One day, while Lauchlan Hamilton was struggling to come up with street names, he came across a handmade map of the area on which the mapmaker had written the word "Heather," presumably because he saw some of the plant growing nearby. With this, Hamilton decided to name all the east-west streets in the area after trees, with the intention being that they'd occur in alphabetical order.

Unfortunately, it doesn't take more than walking a block to learn that these streets are not, in fact, in alphabetical order. After "Ash" comes "Heather," and after "Heather," "Willow." What happened?

Before leaving town on a trip, Hamilton passed the plan on to a draughtsman for the drawing. When he returned, Hamilton discovered, to his horror, that the drawing had been completed and the alphabetical order had been forgotten. It was too late to change the names, and they stuck.

Uncooperative Landowners

The street-naming process would have gone much faster, too, if it weren't for those meddling landowners. If you're wondering why many streets in the downtown core change names partway along, it's because Lauchlan Hamilton couldn't get certain landowners to agree to extend east-west streets through their properties.

This disagreement is also why streets such as Hastings and Pender turn at an angle as they intersect with Cambie. Hamilton wanted the streets in even, straight lines, forming a tidy grid, but a property owner named Pratt refused to go along with the plans.

WRONG TURNS

Angus Angst

In 1912, a lengthy street in Point Grey was given the name
Angus Street, after wealthy landowner and CPR director Richard
Bladworth Angus. One year later, another street nearby was
named Angus Avenue. Unfortunately, these two roads eventually
met up with one another, leading to confusion and inconsistencies,
as many people called portions of each street by the wrong names.

To clear up the confusion, the entire stretch was renamed Angus Drive in 1925. When someone realized that nearby Angus Road was also going to cause some befuddlement, its name was changed to 45th Avenue. Good idea.

Broadway Flop

Broadway Street was given its title in 1909 in anticipation of the street becoming the great centre of a metropolis like New York City's Broadway. Broadway was to intersect with Main Street, which was given its name for the same reason. However, Vancouver grew differently, and Main Street wound up being much less "main" than city council had anticipated. The members of the Street Naming Committee tried to rename Main Street all through the 1940s, but they couldn't seem to muster enough public support. Of course, there were slightly more pressing matters at the time, such as the war.

Scott Street

Several Vancouver streets—Dinmont, Durward, Glengyle, Ivanhoe, Marmion, Midlothian, Nigel, Peveril, Robsart, Talisman, Waverley and Woodstock—are taken from the books of Scottish novelist Sir Walter Scott. One assumes that Scott Street is named after him as well. So how did this happen? It seems that William B. Young, a member of the city's engineering staff who had some say in much of the city planning in the early 1900s, was a fan of Scott's work. It's a shame Young wasn't into *Star Wars*. Vancouver needs an Ackbar Avenue.

Point Grey Secedes, Succeeds

The streets in the Point Grey area, which are numbered, don't always line up with those in the surrounding areas. Why? Point Grey seceded from South Vancouver in 1908. The place was full of upper-class Westerners who wanted higher taxation to improve the streets and sewers. The Easterners didn't agree, however, and the two municipalities split. However, when South Vancouver's development was deemed inefficient and haphazard while Point Grey's looked tidy and measured, the argument was effectively settled. Now Point Grey is one of the wealthiest, tidiest areas in Vancouver.

Golfers? Really?

Before 1966, the only street name drawn from the local First Nations languages was Kitsilano. In 1966, however, the Musqueam, Squamish and Tsleil-Waututh councils objected to the street names in the new Musqueam Park subdivision being named after well-known professional golfers Benjamin Colk and Tony Lema, as the city had first suggested because the park was adjacent to the Shaughnessy golf course. The streets were instead called Halss, Semana, Sennock Crescent, Kullahan Drive and Tamath, after the former Musqueam settlements.

DID YOU KNOW?

Aisne Street, named for the three battles of the Aisne fought on the Aisne River, was officially known as Aines Street, a misspelling, for five years, from 1914 to 1919.

Battle Roads

In 1907, a number of streets in West Vancouver were renamed after famous battles, at the suggestion of alderman T.H. Calland. Alma, Balaclava, Blenheim, Trafalgar and Waterloo streets are the results of this silly idea.

Backwards Activity on Adanac Street

Adanac Street, named in 1930, has an interesting history. Mary Ann Galbraith, an activist, took offence to the disreputable activities —drinking, gambling, prostitution—that were going on along several seedy blocks on the east end, originally known as Union Street. Unwilling to let the good reputation of the Union be dragged through the mud in this way, she led a campaign to call this section Adanac, which is "Canada" spelled backwards. The efforts worked, although the activities didn't stop. But no one thought less of the Union, so maybe Galbraith succeeded.

NAMESAKES

Avison Way

Avison Way, a private thoroughfare in Stanley Park, originally didn't even have a name. Most folks felt it didn't need one, either, since it's really just a road that navigates the park. But the Vancouver Public Aquarium, which is situated in Stanley Park, disagreed. Aquarium management pointed out that it was becoming increasingly difficult to tell postal workers where to bring their mail (and, one assumes, fish), and formally requested that the street be given a name. "Avison" was chosen in honour of Henry Avison, who served as the first employee of the parks board through the 1880s, cutting trails and making roads. His son, Henry Stanley, was the first white child born in the park.

Beechie Is Just Peachy

Not many streets in Vancouver are named after women, but Beatrice "Beechie" Elvina, the daughter of a rich landowner, used to have two of them. She married W.A. Munro, a wealthy businessman who had enough clout to name a street after her given name and another for her nickname. Beechie Street disappeared during rezoning, but Beatrice Street remains.

Boundary Road

Boundary Road was so creatively named because it operated as the boundary line between the City of Vancouver and the municipality of South Vancouver.

Cromwell Street

Cromwell Street, a small road between Marine Way and Kent Street South, was officially renamed Battison Street in 1921. But no one cared—maps in the 1930s continued to list it as Cromwell.

Bentley Street

Most Vancouverites assume Bentley Street is named after the automobile, but it's not, at least not directly. Rather, the street is named after Leopold Bentley, the vice president of a Canadian forest products company. As it turns out, he changed his family name from "Bloch-Bauer" to "Bentley," in honour of the automobile, when he and his family came from Germany in 1938, so there you go.

DID YOU  KNOW?

Leopold Bloch-Bauer, the son of one of Austria's best female equestrian riders, was arrested and jailed when the Nazis seized Austria in 1938. However, the head of the Gestapo was a fan of his mother and allowed Bloch-Bauer to escape, gather his family and flee the country.

Bursill Street

Bursill Street was named in 1913 for John Francis Bursill, a writer who founded the Bursill Library and Collingwood Institute. Bursill was a strange, highly literate man who founded the Vancouver Dickens Fellowship and the Shakespeare society. He also wrote and staged a musical about the history of Vancouver titled "How a Forest Becomes a City" and penned columns for Vancouver's newspapers under the bizarre pseudonym of Felix Penne.

Commercial Street Could Use a Few Commercials

Commercial Street is thusly called because city planners expected great commercial growth in the area following a real estate boom. Everybody was gonna get rich! Unfortunately, it didn't quite happen that way, and when the Garibaldi Centennial Celebration Committee suggested a stretch of Commercial be renamed Garibaldi, the miserly merchants on the drive objected because it would cost them money to get their addresses changed.

DID YOU KNOW?

Trounce Alley sounds like a violent place, but its origins are quite pleasant. It shares its title with an alley in Victoria that was visited by a man named Frank W. Hart. He so enjoyed his visit to the pleasant strip, which contains some of Victoria's best shops and cafes, that he raved about it nonstop, earning the nickname "Hart of Trounce Alley." In Vancouver, he owned a store that backed onto an alley, and it was soon assumed that his nickname came from the name of the alley behind him. It stuck.

Discovery Street

In 1951, it was suggested that Imperial Street be christened Coronation Street to commemorate the coronation of Queen Elizabeth; after all, Canada was part of the Commonwealth. However, residents rejected the suggestion and asserted their independence by giving the street a name with a strong tie to them, rather than the Empire. They settled on Discovery Street, in honour of *Discovery*, the ship of Captain George Vancouver.

The Road to Sainthood

You will find both George Street and St. George Street in Vancouver. Why did one road achieve the distinction of sainthood? Because of the need to tell them apart. In the early 1900s, city authorities realized they had accidentally given two separate streets the same name, so they sainted one.

DID YOU KNOW?

Misspellings were not uncommon among street names. Bidwell Street, for example, was named by Lauchlan Hamilton after a bay from a map he was using in assigning street names. But he was either working too fast or he'd been at it too long that day, because the bay is called Bedwell. The worst misspelling, however, has to be Lockin Street, which gets its name from a man named Henry Lovekin Edmonds. That one's not even close.

Leg-in-a-Boot Square

This creatively named street, appointed in 1976, stems from an incident in 1887 in which a leg in a boot, minus the body, was found in the forest at False Creek. Hoping someone would claim the disembodied leg, the police hung it up outside the police station for two weeks. Unfortunately, nobody wanted the leg, and the man to whom this leg belonged remains a mystery.

Satao Avenue

Although Vancouver has the largest Chinese population of any city in North America, the city didn't see its first Chinese street name, Satao Avenue, until 1996. It's a private thoroughfare named for the landowner.

William Street

William Street was referred to as the "street of indecision" because of its differing street signs. In 1964, 21 signs said "William Street," 22 said "Williams Street" and eight said "Williams East."

Architecture

You don't think your way through a building.

–Arthur Erickson, architect

BIG BUILDINGS, TALL TALES

Vancouver's first skyscraper was the Dominion Building, built in 1909. Clearly the citizens liked the concept. Over the next 100 years, the city skyline has become crowded with remarkable, unique architecture, old-style and new.

After the Dominion Building came the Sun Tower in 1911. Then the Hotel Vancouver in 1916. The remarkable Marine Building showed up in 1929. Another edition of the Hotel Vancouver opened 10 years after that.

In the 1970s, the city added its two tallest buildings: the beautiful Royal Centre and the iconic, extraterrestrial-looking Harbour Centre.

In the first decade of the new millennium, six of the city's 10 tallest buildings opened, including Living Shangri-La, a 201-metre, futuristic masterpiece that looks like it's from another world (which made it an excellent set piece for the movie Tron).

And the city isn't done. Rumour has it the local restrictions on skyscraper height are being renegotiated, and plans for skyscrapers that scrape ever more sky will be drawn up the moment these restrictions change. Vancouver's not gonna stop. The city likes big buildings and it cannot lie.

The War of Light and Dark

When it opened in 2001, the dazzling, elliptical Sheraton Wall Centre was the tallest building in Vancouver. At 137 metres high—48 storeys—it was an imposing and impossible-to-miss piece of the city's landscape. It was also controversial because it wasn't the building architect Peter Wall initially drew up.

The Centre featured a curious blend of light and dark glass, the result of a battle between Peter Wall and the city. Wall planned to use dark glass, and though city officials initially agreed to it, they changed their minds when the windows began to be installed. Corresponding lawsuits followed as the city sued Wall and Wall countersued before a compromise was reached: the bottom 30 floors would contain dark glass, and the top 18 floors light glass.

But Wall added a little extra touch to ensure he won the day. He installed dark blinds on the light-coloured windows that, when closed, mimic the dark panes below. As a result of this, during any bright afternoon, the top 18 storeys are freckled with dark patches.

Don't Trust the Dominion Trust

Few buildings had a shorter first run than the Dominion Trust building, located at the corner of Hastings and Cambie. At the time of its completion in 1910, the 13-storey structure was the tallest commercial building in the British Empire and widely held as Vancouver's first skyscraper. It was built by some of Vancouver's wealthiest businessmen, including Alvo von Alvensleben, who was later arrested for being a German spy. Unfortunately, the building's financiers were soon bankrupted, and in 1914, only four years after Dominion Trust opened, it was closed.

What happened? The building cost a lot, and its financiers were expecting to recoup their losses in real estate and business holdings to the north: a line of the Grand Pacific Railway was to be built to Prince Rupert, promising a major development, but it never came to fruition because the company's president, Charles Hays, died in the sinking of the *Titanic*.

This financial crisis affected other city institutions as well. One of the major tenants of the Dominion Trust was the first Bank of Vancouver, which had only recently begun printing its own money. (Before 1935, it was legal for Canadian banks to do this.) But with the building and the financiers going under, the bank soon did the same, leaving behind only $325,000 in Vancouver bank notes. Needless to say, these notes are now collectors' items.

One popular urban legend states that the building's architect was murdered at the building by the financiers for designing such a pricey structure in 1910. Others have said that he accidentally fell down the stairs during the inspection tour. How did he really die? In his bed, of natural causes, in 1919.

God Is My Civic Planner

There are many beautiful old churches in downtown Vancouver, but few people would disagree that the most incredible of them all is Christ Church Cathedral at 690 Burrard Street. The church was built in the Gothic revival style that was popular at the end of the 19th century and is impossible to miss on a stroll through the downtown area.

Although the building didn't open until 1895, the first Anglican services took place in the basement in 1889. It became a cathedral for the New Westminster diocese in 1929.

For over 100 years, the cathedral has been a major centre in Vancouver religious life. The Royal Family visited the church when they came to Vancouver in 2002. Many of the stained glass windows were paid for by families who had lost loved ones in the World Wars.

In 1970, there was a plan to tear down the church and erect a highrise office tower in its place. Thankfully, this suggestion came during the decade when Vancouver was looking to preserve much of its heritage, and Christ Church Cathedral was definitely that. The outcry against tearing down the church was strong enough that the proposed highrise went up across the street instead, ironically at 666 Burrard Street.

DID YOU KNOW?

The Royal Visit to Vancouver in 2002 marked the first time a reigning monarch had dropped a ceremonial puck at a hockey game. Accompanied by Wayne Gretzky, Queen Elizabeth did exactly that before a pre-season game between the Vancouver Canucks and the San Jose Sharks.

The Marine Building Sinks

The Marine Building was intended to invoke "some great crag rising from the sea, tinted in sea-green, touched with gold," according to its architects. It features a unique, wedding cake "icing" top, and an array of intricately carved ocean creatures.

Originally designed as Vancouver's signature skyscraper, its own-ers soon discovered that their vision was an expensive one, and when the final cost came in at $2.3 million—$1.1 million over budget (during the Great Depression, no less)—they were bankrupted.

At 97.8 metres tall, the Marine was the tallest building in the city until 1939. It was even built with an observation deck that, for 25 cents, provided a breathtaking view of the harbour. Unfortunately, 25 cents was too rich for most people during the Depression, and the deck was closed within only a few months.

Up for sale shortly thereafter, the Marine sold for less than one million dollars. Now it's worth over $25 million.

The building has been used as a location for a great many film projects, most notably, *Timecop, Blade: Trinity,* and *Fantastic Four.* It also was the Daily Planet headquarters on the TV series *Smallville.*

Vancouver Public Library

The main branch of Vancouver's Public Library opened in 1995, and it's a beautiful building, with coliseum-style architecture and an inviting courtyard that is a popular gathering place for members of the community.

It's a snooty building, however, in that it has its back to the other big civic structures surrounding it, notably the Post Office, the Queen Elizabeth Theatre and the CBC Building.

This design was a last-minute shift. Originally, the library was designed to face the other way, but just after the plans were approved, somebody noted the direction of the sun. Facing in the proposed direction, the plaza would have been in the shadow of the building all day, making the place cold, gloomy and uninviting. Hoping to attract more than mopes and vampires, architect Moshe Sadfie turned the map and the frowns of its potential visitors upside-down.

More Depressing Than Regular School

Located atop Burnaby Mountain, Simon Fraser University's iconic design was the victorious entry from an architectural competition held in 1963. The winner was a young professor from the University of British Columbia named Arthur Erickson, who proposed a design inspired by the acropolis in Athens. The uniquely modernist concrete structure has received numerous architectural awards over the years and launched Erickson into prominence as one of Canada's best-known architects.

With its uniquely futuristic Academic Quadrangle and W.A.C. Bennett Library, the campus is a favourite location for science fiction filmmakers. It was first used for the 1972 science fiction film *The Groundstar Conspiracy* and has since been featured in *The Day the Earth Stood Still*, *The 6th Day*, and television programs such as *Stargate SG-1* and *Battlestar Galactica*.

While Simon Fraser University makes filmmakers in search of great locations happy, it can be an incredibly depressing walk on a rainy day. On a dreary day, the grey concrete walls, the dark, depressing halls and lack of colour give the campus the distinct feeling of a prison. The psychological impact that the building can have has fuelled a myth that SFU has the highest suicide rate in Canada. It's not true, but once you've spent a foggy day on Burnaby Mountain, you can see why so many people buy the rumour.

Renovated Gallery

It was only fitting that renowned architect Arthur Erickson take on the responsibility of renovating the Vancouver Art Gallery. The building he renovated was designed in 1906 by Francis Rattenbury, who rose to prominence the exact same way.

Rattenbury got his start in 1892 at just 25, when he came to British Columbia from Leeds, England, and won the right to design Victoria's legendary Parliament Buildings. He went on to win a number of other contracts, among them the commission to design Vancouver's provincial courthouse. In 1980, Arthur Erickson was commissioned to help turn that courthouse into the Vancouver Art Gallery, a renovation that cost $20 million.

The art gallery brings in money in several unusual ways (for example, every Thursday is "cheap date night" with admission by donation, after 5:00 PM), but arguably the strangest way the gallery raises money is by loaning out art pieces. Gallery members can rent paintings, photographs and sculptures to adorn their homes for a month at a time. The rental fees are surprisingly affordable and are tax-deductible for businesses.

DID YOU KNOW?

Francis Rattenbury's death remains an oft-examined case study to this day. In 1925, at the age of 58, he left his wife and children for 27-year-old Alma Pakenham, and two years later the couple returned to England. A decade later, Alma began an affair with their 18-year-old chauffeur, who murdered Rattenbury by striking him repeatedly with a carpenter's mallet. Initially, Alma confessed to the murder, but the chauffeur later admitted he had killed the architect. Many believed that she had pressured the young man to do it. There was a trial and he was sent to prison. Alma was acquitted, only to commit suicide a few days later.

ODD STRUCTURES

Bizarro Hotel

What makes the Winters Hotel such a unique piece of architecture can't be seen from the outside. Built in historic Gastown in 1907—well before modern building codes were established—the hotel contains some of the oddest and most unsettling interiors anywhere. Rooms have enclosed courtyards, windows that overlook hallways rather than, say, the outside, and skylights illuminate many of the hallways.

Some of the rooms are also home to original antique furnishings from when the building first opened, but unfortunately, the current owner has been selling them off in favour of more modern decor.

Still, if you end up in the right room, you'll get the chills. The building isn't haunted, but some corners of it are so disorienting that it's easy to feel as though it might be.

No Site Plan? No Problem!

Built in 1889, making it the oldest building in Vancouver's Chinatown, the Wing Sang Building is full of quirks. For example, the main floor of the building is a few steps down from the street, because it was built before that street had been paved. The second floor is where all second floors should be—above the first—but it's not without its curiosities, either. One door opens to an almost two-storey drop into the alley behind. For obvious reasons, this door is kept locked.

The reason for this drop is that the 40,000-square-foot building was extended twice in the early 1900s, so that it now covers four lots and is essentially two buildings fused together. The building in the front is three storeys high; the one in the back is six storeys.

Getting into the rear building is a chore. You can't see it from the front, because a small wooden facade blocks off the alley that leads to it. To enter, you have to go through the alley to the west or take the elevated walkway on the third floor of the front building, which, for whatever reason, will spit you out on the rear fourth floor.

The building was built by Canadian Pacific Railway employee Yip Sang, a Chinese immigrant who worked for the CPR and the Kwong On Wo company that imported many of the railway's Chinese labourers. Sang intended the building as a house for his family, but it soon became Chinatown's commerce centre, housing an unofficial bank and travel agency through which immigrants could send money or simply arrange passage back home.

Yip is a major Chinese icon in Vancouver, where he used the wealth he accrued to ensure the growing immigrant population had food and shelter. He co-founded the Chinese Benevolent Association and built two buildings—one seven storeys, the other eight—designed to house members of the Chinese community.

DID YOU  KNOW?

Yip Sang's son, Dock Yip, became Canada's first Chinese lawyer in 1945 and took on his father's heart for his people. In 1947, he was instrumental in repealing the Chinese Exclusion Act of 1923, opening the doors for further Chinese immigration into Canada.

Dracula Probably Lives Here

The oldest-looking building in Vancouver has to be Buntzen Lake Powerhouse, Vancouver's first source of hydroelectric power. The building was built in 1914, but it looks like it's about 500 years old and would be the first place I'd look if I was on the hunt for vampires. It's a creepy, old, tumbledown castle-like structure, full of broken windows and faded grandeur, best seen from the water as you travel up Indian Arm.

Although the building looks as abandoned as a bad idea, it's not for sale or for rent, and no mad scientists or super villains squat in it. It's actually still a part of the power grid. Every so often, water will even come streaming out of the gates at the bottom of the building, so it's not just spooky—it's also shocking. (That was a bad pun. Let's move on.)

The Little Church that Couldn't

Vancouver's smallest church was also its most controversial. Dennis Oppenheim's *Device to Root Out All Evil*, a unique, six-metre-tall sculpture of a New England–style chapel balancing upside-down on its steeple, came to the city in 2005 after debuting at the 1997 Venice Biennale. Although the piece was a clear commentary on religion, Oppenheim insists it isn't anti-religious, its name chosen specifically to reflect this. Still, it ruffled feathers everywhere, and the *Device* struggled to find a home. It was even rejected by Stanford University, Oppenheim's alma mater, in 2004. A year later, the Benefic Foundation, a group of Vancouver lawyers that specialize in philanthropy, purchased the sculpture for $300,000. It was unveiled at the Vancouver Sculpture Biennale.

It continued to offend in Vancouver.

Two groups were especially bothered by it, albeit for entirely different reasons. Condo residents in the waterfront area complained the sculpture blocked their view of Coal Harbour. Religious groups claimed the inverted church with its buried steeple was blasphemous. After three years of griping from the rich and religious, the Vancouver Public Parks Committee decided displaying the sculpture was more trouble than it was worth and voted to have it removed.

But the *Device* found a good home. Calgary's Glenbow Museum and the Torode Group of Companies jumped at the chance to host an original Oppenheim on display in their city and paid $100,000 to have the unique piece loaned to them.

LANDMARKS

The Big W

It's not always the brightest idea to walk through Vancouver's downtown Eastside, which is home to some of the city's more unsavoury denizens, but if you do, you might catch the building whose roof holds a big letter "W" sitting atop a mini Eiffel Tower.

That building, which is now empty and remains a topic of great debate among Vancouver's business and social housing groups, was once the site of Vancouver's prominent Woodward's department store.

Charles Woodward was a savvy Vancouver businessman who opened the first Woodward's on the corner of Westminster and Harris. By 1903, the store was a staple, but Vancouver's population had grown to over 13,000, and a larger store was needed. Woodward built a second location on the corner of Abbott and Hastings.

Nine days after the new Woodward's opened, the first one was closed, and for the next 50 years, the Woodward's on Hastings was a fixture of Vancouver's retail scene. The building saw 14 additions over this time, taking over an entire city block of the downtown Eastside. In 1929, the tower with the giant "W" was installed, although the letter was initially at the bottom and a searchlight rested at the top. It was said you could see the light from Vancouver Island.

Twenty-seven years later, in 1956, the red neon "W" was placed atop the tower. While the company has since gone out of business (with many of its locations sold to and now inhabited by the Hudson's Bay Company), the flagship Woodward's building and its "W" persist to this day.

Burrard Street Bridge

The Burrard Bridge is a masterpiece of design—a beautiful, five-lane, Art Deco–style, steel-truss bridge constructed in the 1930s that connects downtown Vancouver with the trendy community of Kitsilano. One of three bridges that crosses False Creek Inlet, Burrard is far and away the most striking and intriguing. The bridge's arches have rooms in them that inspire a lot of questions. Namely, what's in them? Not much, as it turns out. They're primarily decorative, although they used to contain the controls for the lights on the bridge. Getting up there was a chore.

The bridge was said to have been initially designed so that a swinging railway bridge could hang beneath it, but this was never installed. Architects have considered installing a walkway or a bicycle lane there, a solution a lot of Vancouverites would likely be amenable to, especially since the high-traffic bridge recently lost an automobile lane to accommodate cyclists. Non-cyclists, who found the bridge congested even before this decision, were less than impressed.

Warehouse Studio

The Warehouse Studio is a music recording facility in Gastown owned by Vancouver-born rock star Bryan Adams, but the building's history extends beyond the laundry list of A-listers who have laid down tracks in the oldest brick building in the city.

Built in the 1880s by the Oppenheimer brothers, prominent Vancouver entrepreneurs and politicians (David Oppenheimer was Vancouver's second mayor), the building was the site of Vancouver's first wholesale grocery business and city hall. The Warehouse also housed a glass factory and storage warehouse. It's amazing to think that, while seemingly nothing gets done at city hall nowadays, 100 years ago, you could get your milk, cheese and windows there!

By the 1990s, however, the building was abandoned and burnt-out by arsonists, and Adams bought it, spending nearly $6 million to restore its original, late-1800s look. As for the interior, well, it's all rock star comfort. The facility contains all the latest high-tech recording and engineering equipment, as well as an editing suite, lounges, multiple kitchens, a video game room and a putting green. AC/DC, Metallica, Nickelback, Nirvana, R.E.M., Shakira, Slayer, and the Tragically Hip are among the musicians who have recorded albums at the studio.

Skinny Building

When the Sam Kee Company bought the land along Pender Street on which Chinatown's Sam Kee Building stands, it was a standard-sized lot that would have suited a standard-sized building. Unfortunately, in 1912, nine years after the land had been purchased, the City of Vancouver widened Pender Street, expropriating 7.3 metres of the above-ground portion of the property, effectively making it impossible to build any sort of commercial building on the property (unless the patrons are two-dimensional). Or so everyone thought. In 1913, Chang Toy, the company's owner, thumbed his nose at the power structure that had paved over his land without consulting him.

He found a pair of architects willing to design a structure that could fit the narrow lot, and they cleverly pulled it off. The Sam Kee Building is just under 1.5 metres deep on its base floor, and the second floor, which juts out into the street, is 1.8 metres deep but remains high enough for parallel parking.

According to the *Guinness Book of Records*, the Sam Kee Building is the shallowest commercial building in the world, although Pittsburgh's Skinny Building disputes this claim. It's an interesting argument—the Skinny Building is just over 1.5 metres wide on all floors, wider than the bottom floor of the Sam Kee but thinner than the second floor.

The Ugliest House in Vancouver

The year 2010 marked the 100th anniversary of one of Vancouver's most divisive houses, the Tait Manson, located in the wealthy neighbourhood of Shaughnessy. The gaudy structure features two massive domes at its entrance, both of which are trimmed with windows all along the face. Some have called it the ugliest house in Vancouver.

The house was built in 1910 by retired lumber magnate William Lamont Tait, who owned a shingle and sawmill along False Creek and made a killing in the area. Although the building's official name is Glen Brae, named after Tait's wife, citizens in the 1930s mocked the big domes by calling it the Mae West house— the domes resemble bosoms.

With his pockets brimming, Tait spared no expense on the mansion. It had 18 rooms, including six bathrooms as well as a ballroom that took up the entire third floor and was underlaid with a flexible layer of seaweed to make the floor seem softer. Glen Brae boasted one of the first elevators in the entire city of Vancouver, installed for Mrs. Tait, who had only one leg. There were stained glass windows, brass chandeliers and a $16,000 (in 1910) embroidery of Victoria Falls. An imposing wrought-iron fence decorated with gold leaf rosettes surrounded the exterior of the mansion and was apparently shipped in from Scotland at a cost of $10,000 (in 1910!).

The Taits lived in the mansion for only 10 years before both passed away, and with no heirs, the city reluctantly took it over. Caring little about what happened to the building, they rented it out cheaply, which attracted some strange tenants: the Vancouver chapter of the Ku Klux Klan. (They were actually the KKKKK —the Vancouver chapter's full name was the Kanadian Knights of the Ku Klux Klan.)

Klan members felt quite empowered by their fancy clubhouse, which they occupied in 1912 for just $150 a month. The group grew to over 5000 members, all of whom paraded around in the beautifully landscaped yard with their white hoods and robes, even staging a cross-burning on the lawn.

The KKK were an annoying and stupid group, and within a year, City Council passed a bylaw that made it illegal to wear a mask in public. One wonders if perhaps the KKK shot themselves in the foot when they set up shop in a neighbourhood full of rich and influential people who were sure to hate them. Within a few weeks of the bylaw, the group had dwindled to 200 members and they left Glen Brae within a year.

Today, the house has better tenants. The Canuck Place Children's Hospice, one of Canada's premier specialized care facilities, now rents the space The hospice is supported by the Vancouver Canucks, and the team's players visit the children on a regular basis.

DID YOU KNOW?

Although the bylaw prohibiting public mask-wearing is no longer in effect, there was a strong push to bring it back after the Vancouver Stanley Cup riots, when prosecution became difficult because several rioters covered their faces.

Movement at City Hall

There's nothing overly strange about the way City Hall looks. It's a beautiful Art Deco building with a 12-storey tower, an eight-foot statue of Captain George Vancouver and a second-floor ceiling made of gold leaf from BC mines. The oddness of it comes from where it's located, at Cambie and West 12th avenue, far from the downtown core.

The location is the bright idea of Gerry McGreer, an enthusiastic politician who ran for mayor of Vancouver in 1934. He ran campaign ads in the *Vancouver Sun* promising to eradicate gambling, white slavery and corruption, as well as start work on a new city hall, largely as a way to create jobs during the Great Depression.

Initially, McGreer's proposal placed the city hall building at Pender and Cambie, right where the action was—two blocks down from Gastown and just down the street from the school that would become Vancouver Community College.

Unfortunately, as the builders were set to begin construction, a Relief Camp Workers' Union (RCWU) protest broke out at the site, with nearly 2000 marching in a "snake parade" (zigzagging, two by two) through the streets. After RCWU members entered the Hudson's Bay Company and began to harass the shoppers, several fights broke out and the situation became heated enough that McGreer had to proclaim the Riot Act in nearby Victory Square.

Not particularly interested in facing more protests, McGreer decided to do something about it: he moved the city hall to a quieter place.

Science World

One of Vancouver's most recognizable landmarks is the giant silver golf ball (in actuality, a geodesic dome) sitting at the end of the False Creek Inlet The dome is home to the Alcan Omnimax theatre, one of the largest dome theatres in the world. The film screen is 27 metres in diameter and five storeys high. The theatre seats

400 people, and a 45-minute film requires about four kilometres of Omnimax film stock.

The dome was built for the 1986 World's Fair and originally named Expo Centre. After the fair, citizens lobbied for the unique structure to be turned into a science centre. In 1988, "Science World" opened.

That's no longer its official name, mind you. On July 20, 2005, Telus purchased the building and renamed it the Telusphere, which led to a massive outcry. Shortly after that, Telus backed off, changing the name to the Telus World of Science. But Vancouverites don't much care for that moniker either; everyone still calls it Science World. Even the SkyTrain stop that drops off passengers across the street from the sphere is called "Science World."

Haunted Vancouver

The more enlightened our houses are,
the more their walls ooze ghosts.

–Italo Calvino, novelist

SPOOKY SITES

You'd think that Vancouver, a relatively young city, would be limited in its ghost stories, but that couldn't be further from the truth. It doesn't take long to find a ghost. All you need is an unsolved death, a building with secrets or an architectural quirk that gets the mind racing. The city is full of those. Hence, it's also full of otherworldly spirits.

From Waterfront Station's "headless brakeman" to Hycroft Mansion's "crying man" to the Fairmont Hotel's "lady in red," Vancouver is home to some solid ghosts (albeit not solid in the literal sense; everybody knows ghosts are translucent). But don't panic if you cross paths with one: few are malicious. They're just out for the attention. If there's one common element among Vancouver's ghost population, it's that they like to be seen. Many seem to intentionally draw attention (one plays the drums, for goodness' sakes!). With that in mind, if ever you see a ghost, the wisest plan of action might be to acknowledge it with a friendly wave and be on you way. Or scream and run.

Mostly Ghostly

Located in Shaughnessy, one of Vancouver's upper-crust neighbour-hoods, Hycroft Mansion is said to be haunted with seven ghosts.

At 20,000 square feet, the massive, 30-room house is exactly the sort of place you'd expect to be haunted. The many secret doors, tunnels, stairways and rooms believed to harbour valuable heirlooms make it chock full of intrigue. Built in the early 1900s by prominent Vancouver investor Duncan McRae, the mansion routinely hosted parties of the rich and famous that spawned rumours of scandal.

During World War II, the building was used as a veterans' hospital after McRae, a former military general whose primary task was purchasing warhorses, basically gave it to the government, selling it for one dollar. Many people have died inside these walls.

Who are the seven ghosts? Several people have reported to seeing an elderly man dressed in a World War I uniform, supposedly Duncan McRae himself. He has often been seen with a woman believed to be his wife. Four of the other ghosts, including a "crying man" that many have heard in one of the rooms on the lower floor, are believed to be World War II veterans. The last ghost is their nurse.

Though the ghosts generally don't make appearances during the many parties and receptions held at the mansion that the University Women's Club of Vancouver now owns, they seem to have something against the film crews that shoot on location at Hycroft, especially those that focus on paranormal activity, such as *The X-Files*. As paranormal entities themselves, perhaps they don't like the way they're being portrayed.

The Headless Brakeman and Other Ghosts

Quite possibly the most haunted building in downtown Vancouver, Waterfront Station is the Western terminus of the CPR. This beautiful heritage site was built in 1915, during an era when train travel was the height of elegance, and the architecture makes that abundantly clear.

The station is one of Vancouver's finest stops. Today, the building is a busy hub that acts as a base for the city's various public transportation systems, including SkyTrain, the SeaBus, the West Coast Express train, city buses and the Helijet to Victoria.

Thousands of people pass through Waterfront Station on a daily basis, and even more if you count all the ghosts. One guard claimed to have seen a flapper from the 1920s dance by herself on the building's west side. Another person claimed to have fled an empty room in the building's northwest corner after seeing a glowing, bright white ghost of a woman stretch her hand toward him. A third story tells of a guard who entered a room that stored a number of old desks, only to have the desks rearrange themselves behind him and block the path to the door.

And phantom footsteps have been heard on the beautiful tiled floors. Many have reported seeing the ghosts of little old ladies on the station bench, waiting for a train that never comes (or maybe simply sharing the latest ghost gossip). Then there's the true story of a brakeman who slipped on the wet railway tracks while making repairs one night by lantern. He was knocked unconscious and was decapitated by a passenger train. Unsurprisingly, many have since claimed to have seen the "headless brakeman" wandering the tracks, lantern in hand, presumably looking for his lost head.

Blood Alley

Perhaps the most appropriately named place in all of Vancouver is Gastown's Blood Alley, which was officially given its name during the 1972 renovation of Gastown. These days, the area is home to excellent restaurants such as the Old Spaghetti Factory and Vancouver's staple, the Salt Tasting Room. One hundred years ago, however, the street was home to a number of butchers, all of whom had no qualms about dumping buckets of their waste into the streets. As a result, the alley was often thick with wet blood.

This activity also made the alley a great place to commit bloodshed without drawing attention to the crime scene. According to local legend, many were robbed and murdered in the alley, fights often took place there, and much of the blood in the streets was human.

But not all the human deaths were unsanctioned. Public executions were done in the square for many of the same reasons: expectations for clean-up were minimal. With all the death associated with Blood Alley, it's not surprising that the entire neighbourhood is presumed to be haunted. The Old Spaghetti Factory has its own stories, but the entire area has been said to carry a horrifying, psychic energy, and many patrons claim to have experienced psychic visions, visitations and seen ghostly apparitions while walking through Blood Alley at night.

Apparitions and Alfredo

The Old Spaghetti Factory is an Italian-style restaurant chain with locations all over North America, but the Gastown location is special. The old-style building blends in perfectly with the historical look of one of the city's major tourist stops. The building is only 40 years old, but you'd think it had been built in the 1800s.

The design is not what gives the place an old feel, however. It's also the ghosts. The Old Spaghetti Factory is said to have two. The first is the spirit of a train conductor believed to have died during an underground collision directly beneath the restaurant. Most of his appearances take place inside of Number 53, an old streetcar that once served as a public transit trolley in New Westminster and now holds dining tables within the restaurant. Kitchen staff have claimed to have seen the conductor quietly sitting at one of the tables after hours, and others have reported cold spots, moving table settings, and in one instance, bent cutlery. Apparently, the conductor doesn't care for forks.

The second ghost, known as the "little red man," is a small, mischievous red-headed man in red long johns and a red shirt (clearly much more brazen than the conductor) who makes appearances in the ladies restroom and strolls through the kitchen. No one knows where he came from or who he is, but he's obviously the ghost of an intrusive pervert.

Haunted Drill Hall

Built in the early 20th century, the drill hall on Beatty Street is Vancouver's oldest such building. Since its construction, the hall has acted as the headquarters and training centre for British Columbia's senior militia regiment, The Duke of Connaught's Own, once a rifle regiment and now a wheeled reconnaissance unit. The militia saw action in both World Wars.

The imposing old building has a foundation of giant granite blocks, a limestone parapet and two round towers flanking the front entrance.

Speaking of imposing, unwanted spectres are said to reside in the hall along with the officers in training. Some claim to have seen the apparition of a man in the mess halls, and many more have reported hearing strange noises, phantom footsteps and items inexplicably falling from shelves and off the walls.

Waiting at The Landing

Situated at 375 Water Street near Gastown, The Landing is
a multi-tenanted commercial building built in the early 1900s that
overlooks the harbour and the cruise ship terminal. Among its
tenants is the "woman in white," a ghostly apparition said to stalk
the hallways and only ever reported as moving in one direction.
Each person who has seen her claims she walks toward the north
window, stops, looks out at the harbour and then vanishes.

She could be waiting for an incoming ship. She could be taking in
the breathtaking view of the sea. Or she could be a legend fabricated
by the building's security guards to scare new hires on their first
graveyard shift.

The Lady in Red

Vancouver is home to a great deal of luxury hotels, and the
Fairmont Hotel Vancouver is considered the cream of the crop,
perhaps in part because of its royal lineage. Construction of
the hotel originally began in 1929, but it slowed because of the
Great Depression. Ten years later, the building was rushed to completion and classed up considerably for the royal visit of King
George VI and Queen Elizabeth, who came to Canada to drum
up support for the impending war with Germany.

Ironically, the royals never stayed in the suite. They arrived in
Vancouver by train on a Monday morning and left for Victoria
late that same afternoon.

The building is full of all sorts of other interesting facts. The top
floor has an old CBC studio that broadcast big band leader Dal
Richards for 25 years. The hotel's roof is green, for whatever reason,
and the building is full of eerie old ducts, water tanks and a massive
chimney stack.

And the 14th floor has two elevators that don't work, except for
the lady in red, Vancouver's most famous ghost, who is said to

hover the hallways, ride the elevators to who knows where and occasionally step out onto window ledges.

But don't be afraid of the lady in red. According to the hotel, which embraces her legend and even uses it in their marketing, she's friendly. They would know—she was a frequent guest even before she died. Her real name is Jennie Pearl Cox, and she was a regular at the hotel's ballroom in the 1930s and 1940s. According to the Fairmont's public relations coordinator, after she was involved in a fatal car crash in 1944, Cox's spirit took up residence in her favourite hotel.

It's a great story, especially since she likes to play tricks on the hotel staff. In other words, if there's a booking conflict, it was probably the ghost.

Hitchhiking Ghost

According to legend, sometime in the 1960s, a couple driving to the UBC campus library on University Boulevard got into an argument. As things got heated, the driver stopped the car and the female passenger got out to walk away, only to be struck dead by a car that failed to see her. Fifty years later, men driving the boulevard claim to have stopped to pick up a hitchhiking woman who hands them a piece of paper with the library's address on it and then suddenly vanishes.

All Cemeteries Are Haunted

This story is a bit of a cheat since pretty much every cemetery is purported to be haunted, but many of the ghosts seen at Mountain View are said to be victims of the sinking of the SS *Princess Sophia*, a coastal passenger liner in the CPR's coastal service fleet. In the worst maritime accident in the history of North America's Pacific Coast, the *Sophia* became stranded along Vanderbilt Reef, a massive rock invisible at high tide, and sunk along the Alaskan coast. All 353 passengers perished in the shipwreck, 66 of whom were buried at Mountain View.

Prior to the opening of the cemetery, white settlers used the island as a burial ground, and in the late 1800s, it was used as a quarantine for those suffering smallpox. Lucky them.

Vogue Theatre

Opened in 1941, the Vogue initially hosted mainly movie showings, but after closing in 1988 and being reopened in 1991 with brand-new lighting and sound systems, it has since become one of Vancouver's most popular live music destinations. Located at thesouth end of the Granville Mall, the Vogue occupies one of the hippest areas in the city, and as a result, it attracts many of the hippest bands.

The theatre also attracted a pretty hip ghost—a tall, dapper man in his mid-thirties dressed in a cream-coloured dinner jacket (even after Labour Day!). The ghost is said to have a long face, dark and chiselled features and a healthy appetite for the arts. He has no compunction about playing the drum kits at night, rearranging the stage props and taking in free performances underneath the exit sign at stage left and from the doorway of the theatre's projection booth. The ghost has traumatized a few tap dancers, terrified more than a handful of stage technicians and appeared to dozens of staff members over the theatre's 70 years.

Shebeen Whisky House

If you're wandering through Gastown late at night looking for a place with some personality to get your drink on, try the Shebeen Whisky House.

In Ireland, a *shebeen* was an illicit dive bar that was home to all kinds of under-the-table liquor sales, and while this bar in Gastown is perfectly legal, it's tucked away enough to seem like a place that has something to hide.

The bar also has something to drink. The Shebeen offers the largest selection of whiskys in BC—more than 100 different kinds, which is heaven for anyone with a passion for single malts, bourbons, ryes, scotch and Irish whisky. No wonder the intimate little bar (it only seats 40) has been visited by plenty of famous people, such as U2, Bob Geldof and Marilyn Manson.

Speaking of visitations, the Shebeen is also said to be home to a mischievous ghost that enjoys knocking glasses and bottles of whiskey off the table and smashing them on the floor. While the sprite can serve as a handy excuse for butterfingers, don't expect people to believe you. According to the owners, he does most of his mischief after the bar is closed.

Sporting Vancouver

If I would have myself passing to me,
I would have 24 goals, too.

–Henrik Sedin, Vancouver Canucks' captain

HOCKEY TOWN

Vancouver isn't known for its championship teams, primarily because it doesn't have many. As it stands, the city has three major sports teams: the Vancouver Canucks, the Vancouver Whitecaps and the BC Lions. Of the three, only the Lions have ever won a championship. For the most part, the city is home to lovable losers.

The Canucks have been the worst of the bunch, which makes it downright incredible that they're basically the only sports team the city truly cares about. While they've been in contention for the Stanley Cup for the last few years, the majority of their 40 seasons have been beyond disappointing. When the team gets close to a championship win and falls short, the city residents simply don't know what to do with themselves. Unfortunately, that usually means a riot.

Maybe it's a product of the provincial obsession with hockey, a violent game, but sports riots are as much a part of Vancouver's history as the Canadian Pacific Railway or Stanley Park. After two embarrassing Stanley Cup riots, the city has a history of losing badly.

The news isn't all bad. The Canucks may not have won a Stanley Cup, but that doesn't mean Vancouver has never been home to a Stanley Cup champion. They have. Furthermore, the city has birthed some other major hockey traditions: towel power, ugly retro jerseys and the Roxy.

And while it's not usually a well-received suggestion, if you look past the Canucks, the city's history contains plenty of *other proud sports moments: the Miracle Mile, the Vancouver Millionaires and the discovery of Pamela Anderson.*

Okay, Vancouver's sporting history is admittedly a mixed bag.

The Shifty Canucks

The Vancouver Canucks have a long history of shady deals, such as the way they came to acquire the rights of Russian speedster Pavel Bure. Selected 113th overall in the sixth round of the 1989 NHL entry draft, Bure was supposed to be ineligible at the time because he hadn't played the required number of professional games in Russia. However, Canucks' scout Mike Penny had discovered some additional exhibition and international games that technically saw Bure meet eligibility requirements, so the team drafted him. The pick was initially deemed illegal, at which point the Canucks produced the game sheets they'd been sitting on.

But perhaps the shiftiest story involving the Canucks is the one behind how they got their name. In 1945, local character Coley Hall wanted to own the new Vancouver hockey team set to join the Pacific Coast Hockey Association, but the franchise had already been awarded to businessman Chuck Charles. So Hall went to Pacific National Exhibition president Mackenzie Bowell and instead snapped up the rights to the place where the team would play. Then Hall shut the team out. With nowhere for his team to play, Charles was forced to hand the Canucks over to Hall.

To celebrate, Hall went to have a drink with Art Nevison, a local bootlegger, and asked him what he should call the team. A fan of comic book hero Johnny Canuck, Nevison replied, "Call them the Canucks."

Towel Power

Ironically, it's a common rallying tactic among sports fans to wave white towels in support of their team, but few know that this curious practice originated with the Vancouver Canucks. The act was a passive protest launched by the famously innovative Roger Nielson, the Canucks' head coach from 1982 to 1984.

Nielson was known for thinking outside the box. Among his most well-known innovations was the use of videotape to analyze other teams, as well as microphone headsets to communicate with his assistant coaches. He was a master of reading the NHL rulebook for loopholes, once instructing his goaltender to leave his stick in the crease when he came to the bench for an extra attacker, preventing the puck from sliding into the unattended goal. On penalty shots, Nielson played a defenseman instead of a goalie, instructing the player to rush out and challenge the shooter. With his team down two men late in a five-on-three, Neilson once sent too many men out on the ice intentionally, knowing his team couldn't be made any more shorthanded.

But the coach's most famous moment came during a 1982 playoff game between the Canucks and the Chicago Blackhawks. Annoyed with what he perceived as refereeing biased against his team, Neilson took a trainer's white towel and casually held it on a hockey stick as a white flag of surrender. Three other players followed suit, and all were ejected from the game for their impudence.

Fans rallied behind the protest, however, showing up to the following game with thousands of white towels of their own, and waving them in vigorous support of their team. The Canucks went on to win the series and made their first appearance in the Stanley Cup final that spring, falling to the New York Islanders in a sweep.

Neilson's towel stunt remains a playoff tradition in Vancouver to this day. In 2010, the Canucks erected a statue commemorating the moment outside of Rogers Arena, where they play.

What's in a Jersey?

Although the Vancouver Canucks have been around for only 41 years, they've gone through a whopping 13 different logo and jersey changes in their history, most of them ill-conceived. While the current Canucks jersey is quite popular, especially as a retro throwback to the colour scheme and look of their debut jerseys in 1970, everything in between has been famously atrocious.

None have been worse than their famous Flying V jerseys, worn from 1978 to 1985. The sweaters featured a huge yellow, red-orange and black striped "V" that began at the shoulders and met at the hem. They are widely held to be the ugliest jerseys not only in NHL history but in all of sports as well.

Vancouver's Lone Stanley Cup

Despite coming within a game of the Stanley Cup championship on two separate occasions, the Canucks remain one of only a handful of NHL organizations that have yet to win the prize. But that's not to say Vancouver has never been home to the Stanley Cup champions. They have.

In 1915, the Vancouver Millionaires of the Pacific Coast Hockey Association (PCHA) won the Stanley Cup in a five-game series with the National Hockey Association's (NHA) Ottawa Senators. It wasn't even close, as the Millionaires won three straight in the

best-of-five series, outscoring the Senators 26–8 over the games to claim the Stanley Cup at home in Vancouver's Denman Arena.

Of course, it helped that the Millionaires boasted the Senators' former star player in Frederick Wellington "Cyclone" Taylor. Taylor was one of hockey's best players and already a Stanley Cup champion with Ottawa in 1909, but he moved to Vancouver in 1912 after being offered $1200 to play there. Though the PCHA and the NHA worked together in 1915 and 1916, allowing the Millionaires a chance at the Cup, the relationship soon turned sour. It's safe to assume the talent-poaching played into the acrimony.

Denman Arena

Built by wealthy hockey legends Frank and Lester Patrick, who did as much to bring hockey to Vancouver as anyone, Denman Arena was Vancouver's first big sports venue. It was built in 1911 at a cost of $300,000—peanuts when you consider that the GM Place scoreboard cost $6 million in 1995. But Denman was a modern masterpiece. The wood and brick building seated 10,500, making it one of the world's largest arenas, and featured one of

Canada's first two artificial ice surfaces. While it was built specifically for the PCHA, the arena also hosted a number of other events. Jack Dempsey, the world heavyweight champion from 1919 to 1926, boxed at the arena in 1931.

The arena harboured some incredible hockey history—it was the site of Vancouver's first official game of hockey on January 5, 1912—but it lost the chance to be declared a heritage site when an explosion at the adjacent Coal Harbour coal shed destroyed it in 1936.

Stanley Cup Riots

The Vancouver Canucks have been to the Stanley Cup final three times in their 40-year history, twice making it all the way to the seventh game of the series. In 1994, led by captain Trevor Linden, goaltender Kirk Maclean and Russian speedster Pavel Bure, the Canucks exceeded all playoff expectations, storming into the final versus the New York Rangers.

The Canucks did their best, pushing the series to the bitter end, but they couldn't overcome captain Mark Messier and the star-studded New York line-up, falling in game seven at Madison Square Garden, 3–2. The loss was disappointing, although not quite as disappointing as what happened next.

Immediately after the game was completed, over 50,000 individuals converged on the downtown Vancouver area, and the situation quickly got out of hand. After a man climbed a lamppost only to fall and suffer an injury, the police—who were on bicycles—tried to disperse the crowd to get paramedics to the man. The crowd immediately got aggressive.

By the time the crowd was finally brought back under control, the riot had caused over $1 million in damage, and up to 200 individuals had been injured.

When the Canucks returned to the Stanley Cup final in 2011 versus the Boston Bruins, fears of another riot had subsided, largely because of the friendly vibe and commendable behaviour the city had demonstrated during the 2010 Vancouver Olympics. Acting on either good faith or foolishness, depending on who you ask, the city installed two large viewing screens in the downtown core and closed off two blocks, allowing Canuck fans to funnel in during the final series.

An estimated 100,000 people packed into the area on the night of game seven. The turnout was overwhelming. The police once again found themselves undermanned, and the crowd was large enough both to prevent emergency vehicles from getting through and to enable people to bring alcohol in unchecked.

When the Boston Bruins won the final game, the scene once again turned violent in a hurry. Within minutes of the loss, Bruins and Canucks flags had been set ablaze, and some rioters overturned a vehicle in front of the Canada Post headquarters. A young man inserted a white towel into the gas tank and lit it on fire. Then full-scale pandemonium ensued.

Vancouver mayor Gregor Robertson, who had okayed the screens that brought in double the amount of people who rioted the last time the Canucks lost the Stanley Cup, attributed the situation to "a small group of troublemakers." Despite his naiveté (as well as providing the understatement of the year), he was re-elected as mayor three months later.

Kissing Couple

While it's hard to argue that anything good came from the riots, one incredibly memorable image was created by the incident: a photo of a young couple lying on the street kissing, blissfully ignorant of the rioters in the background and a member of the riot police in the foreground. The bizarre photo went viral within hours of being posted to the Getty Images database amid rumours that it had been staged. It hadn't.

The young woman in the photo was knocked down by riot police trying to calm the crowd, and she had twisted her ankle. Her boyfriend had laid down beside her while they waited for help and was merely trying to comfort her. Still, the image looks like something out of a poster for a post-apocalyptic movie.

Freelance photographer Rich Lam, hired by the *Vancouver Sun* to take photos at the game, snapped the now-iconic picture while moving away from the riot. He had no idea what he'd done until he returned to the *Vancouver Sun* offices and turned his camera's memory card over to his editor.

Roxy Flu

For over 20 years, the Roxy has been one of Vancouver's most popular nightclubs and for years it was especially popular among NHL players. The beer-and-whisky joint is so renowned as a hockey haunt that Vancouverites have a term for sluggish play after a night on the town: "The Roxy Flu."

For whatever reason, hockey players love the Roxy. It's such a popular hangout for NHLers that coaches often forbid their players from frequenting it during visits to Vancouver, and others use it as motivational tool. *Win tonight, boys, and you can go to the Roxy.*

The Roxy Flu has never been officially proved as a real malady, but its effects has been observed multiple times. Teams that fly into Vancouver the day before games often put in half-hearted performances, and many of Vancouver's nightlife enthusiasts are quick to tell you who they spotted in the VIP section of the Roxy the night before a game.

After home wins, Canuck players are often asked about the "Roxy Effect" and whether they think it factored into the victory. Recently, Canucks' centre Ryan Kesler was queried on that very subject. He said, "We're a good team and we earn those wins, but maybe the Roxy makes a game a bit more one-sided or slows a team down enough that they can't come into our building and steal one."

PIGSKIN PICKS

Turfed

On January 5, 2007, Vancouverites everywhere thought they heard thunder, or maybe a parade of elephants. What they actually heard was the inflatable roof of BC Place stadium collapsing under the weight of wind, rain and snow.

This episode was just the most recent in the history of a building that had been nothing but a headache since it was built in 1983 at a cost of $100 million. While the indoor facility, home to the BC Lions, was attractive at first, fans stopped enjoying watching football indoors and attendance dropped off sharply. Worse, the Lions weren't all that good, and as their drawing power diminished, BC Place became home to poorly attended CFL games, car shows and trade fairs. It was enough to make some wonder why the stadium had even been built in the first place, especially since the Lions were only ever going to play eight home games there a year.

But a plan had been in place when the stadium went up: it was originally supposed to attract a baseball team. Unfortunately, the turf, which was hard and uneven, was a turn-off, as was the roof. Baseballs fans, like football fans, prefer to watch their games outdoors.

With that in mind, the collapsed roof was something of a blessing, although taxpayers didn't think so. Unwilling to demolish the building, the provincial government okayed a $563-million renovation focused around installing a retractable roof. The updated BC Place stadium opened on September 30, 2011, only two months before the BC Lions went on a late-season tear and won the Grey Cup at home...with the roof closed. There was a threat of precipitation, and the expensive roof has one major flaw: for whatever reason, it can't close in the rain.

The Vancouver Whitecaps—Vancouver's Major League Soccer team—now play there, and with a roof that opens, the city hasn't given up hope on getting a baseball team.

DID YOU KNOW?

Perhaps the most embarrassing moment in BC Place's early history came when Edgar Martinez, one of the leading hitters for the Seattle Mariners, tore his hamstring when he tripped over an unzipped seam in the turf during an exhibition game in 1993. Martinez didn't retire for another 10 years, but he only played as a designated hitter. He never played in the field again.

The Grey Cup Riots

Decades before the Stanley Cup riots of 1994 and 2011, Vancouver sports fans demonstrated the miserable hooliganism they were capable of, rioting multiple times in the 1960s, during which BC hosted five Grey Cups.

The 1963 riot that followed the hometown Lions losing the Grey Cup game to the Hamilton Tiger-Cats 21–10 was the worst riot in Vancouver history up to that point. Fans were upset not just with the outcome of the game but also a nasty hit by Tiger-Cats' linebacker (and later pro wrestler) Angelo Mosca on Lions' running back Willie Fleming. Fleming was injured on the hit and left the game for the hospital immediately.

After the game, someone threw a bottle in frustration, striking a woman in the head. As the police moved through the crowd to find the culprit, the crowd bristled at their intrusion and lashed out, hurling bottles, rocks, eggs and tomatoes at the officers and turning the area near Granville and Georgia into a battlefront. Police arrested 319 people.

The 1966 riot was nearly as bad, with almost 200 people arrested before the game even started and another 100 by the time the riot finally wound down.

It should be noted, however, that the fans weren't the only ones who acted poorly as a result of these games. Just before the 2011 Grey Cup, which was also held in Vancouver, former Lion Joe Kapp, Vancouver's quarterback from 1961 to 1965, was invited to a luncheon with Mosca in attendance. The two men were invited up to the stage, and when Kapp arrived, he extended Mosca a flower from one of the table centrepieces. Mosca responded by telling him, "Shove it up your ass." When Kapp instead tried to shove the flower up Mosca's nose, Mosca swung his cane in retaliation, and the two 73-year-olds traded kicks and punches until Mosca fell behind the stage and the fight was broken up.

DID YOU  KNOW?

The BC Lions are the only CFL team whose city appears nowhere in their name. It's strange, especially since the team's nickname is based on The Lions, a twin mountain peak that can be seen from Vancouver and looks like two lions guarding the city.

Did D.B. Cooper Attend the Grey Cup?

The mystery surrounding legendary dastard D.B. Cooper, who perpetrated the only unsolved airplane hijacking in U.S. history on November 24, 1971, continues to baffle investigators 40 years later. Boarding a plane at Portland International Airport, Cooper claimed that he had a bomb that would be set off if he wasn't given $200,000 in ransom, four parachutes and a fresh tank of fuel for the jet upon landing. When his demands were met, Cooper released the passengers and ordered the pilots take the plane to Mexico.

Cooper is believed to have jumped from the plane while it flew over the Washington wilderness, and many speculated that he may have gone north, rather than south, escaping into Vancouver, at least for a time.

Six days after the hijacking and one day after the CFL's 59th Grey Cup, when both events were big news in the Vancouver papers, a man calling himself D.B. Cooper wrote a brief letter to the chief editor of *The Province* that read: "The composite drawing [of D.B. Cooper] on Page 3 as suspected by the FBI does not represent the truth. I enjoyed the Grey Cup game. Am leaving Vancouver. Thanks for your hospitality. D.B. Cooper."

Pamela Anderson Gets Noticed

D.B. Cooper wasn't the only beguiling personality to have been a noteworthy attendee of a CFL game. That's where buxom former *Baywatch* babe, Playboy playmate and early viral video star Pamela Anderson was discovered. She was, after all, a great deal easier to spot than Cooper.

In 1989, 21-year-old Anderson attended a Lions game at BC Place in a form-fitting Labatt beer T-shirt and was spotted by a camera operator who felt her worthy of a moment on the JumboTron. The moment she appeared on the screen, the crowd reportedly broke into one of the loudest cheers in the team's history. But where some saw a lovely local, the Labatt company saw a readymade marketing tool, and within days she was signed as "The Blue Zone Girl," the company's official spokesperson.

DID YOU KNOW?

The connection between the Canucks and the Lions persists beyond the fact that both sports have seen riots. The autumn after both the 1994 and 2011 Stanley Cup riots, the Grey Cup was hosted by the city of Vancouver, and the BC Lions won it both times.

OTHER SPORTS

The Vancouver Grizzlies Were Terrible

One Vancouver sports team that never incited a riot was the Vancouver Grizzlies, the NBA franchise the city briefly hosted between 1995 and 2001. It seems that to incite crowds to riot in Vancouver, a team has to fall short of a championship. Lucky for the authorities, the Grizzlies never even came close.

Fans were optimistic after the team's first two games, both of which were wins, but after that, reality set in. The Grizzlies lost their next 19 games, and later set the NBA single-season record with 23 consecutive losses from February to April. They ended the season with 15 wins and 67 losses.

The terrible team never improved, largely because it also suffered from terrible management. The team drafted players with no interest in playing in Vancouver, such as Steve Francis, who publicly stated prior to his selection that he wouldn't play in the city.

Ludicrous contracts were handed out, such as the one to Bryant "Big Country" Reeves who routinely showed up for training camp overweight and was as slow a player as there was in the NBA. At times, the team seemed to have no idea what it wanted. Over the Grizzlies' first four seasons in Vancouver, they won a grand total of 56 games, a number that good NBA teams reach annually.

Fans were done with the Grizzlies by the time NBA players went on strike in 1998, and when the strike was resolved in early 1999, Vancouverites had learned to live without the team and they stopped attending the games. The team was sold and moved to Memphis two years later.

Olympic Concerns

In 2010, Vancouver became the third Canadian city to host the Olympics after Montréal in 1976 and Calgary in 1988, and you'd be hard-pressed to find somebody who might claim it wasn't a rousing success.

There were some serious hiccups early on, however. The heavy rain and warm temperatures at Cypress Mountain threw the status of some of the alpine events into question, and snow had to be trucked in from nearby Manning Park. During the opening ceremonies, one of the four mechanical arms of the indoor torch malfunctioned, never rising from the floor. But far and away the most unfortunate was the death of Georgian luger Nodar Kumaritashvili, who lost control of his luge during a practice run hours before the opening ceremony. It was one of only five deaths to have ever occurred at the Olympic Winter Games, the second in the luge event.

In the first few days of the Games, British Columbians were beginning to wonder why they had voted to host the darn Olympics. BC had, after all, been the first place in Olympic history to stage a civic vote for the Games and emerge in favour of it. The Olympics had been vetoed two times prior, both of which have a curious connection to Vancouver. In the 1970s, the people of

Colorado defeated their state's plan to host the Summer games, dropping out unexpectedly. When they did, organizers quietly asked if Vancouver would like to host, but the provincial government declined the request. The second failed plebiscite came in Switzerland in 2010, when the people of Bern voted against the Games and the nation dropped their bid. Vancouver wound up hosting, but in the opening days, it seemed like a mistake.

Public opinion turned sharply when Alexander Bilodeau, a freestyle skier, won Canada's first gold medal, which was also the first Olympic gold medal ever won during a Canadian games. Until then, Canada had been the only Olympic host country to emerge from its own Games without a gold, and it had done it twice. With that obstacle finally overcome, Canadians won medals in record numbers, picking up 14 golds, more than any other country, and 26 medals total.

One of those golds came in men's ice hockey, the marquee event of the tournament, after Sidney Crosby scored the game-winning goal in overtime. It instantly became one of the most memorable goals in Canadian hockey history.

Get into a Game of Ultimate

Vancouver sports teams aren't typically the cream of the crop, but when it comes to the sport of Ultimate, a game not unlike football that uses 175-gram flying discs (often the Frisbee brand), Vancouver's teams are the best. That's because, unbeknownst to many, Ultimate is Vancouver's largest team sport.

The Vancouver Ultimate League Society, a non-profit group that facilitates league play throughout the city, has over 4000 active members playing for any one of 200 official teams and eight organized leagues. Vancouver teams have won multiple national championships, and the city is known nationwide for producing some of the best Ultimate players in Canada.

The Miracle Mile

On May 6, 1954, during a track meet at Oxford, British runner Roger Bannister became the first person to run a mile in under four minutes, finishing the race in 3:59.4. It was a feat that many thought was impossible, but just 46 days later in Turku, Finland, Bannister got word that Australian runner John Landy had beaten the record by an entire second. For the first time in the world, two men were capable of running a mile in less than four minutes.

Fans of track and field didn't have to wait long to see the athletes go head to head, as both runners appeared at the August 1954 British Empire and Commonwealth Games in Vancouver in a race billed as "The Miracle Mile." The race remains the most famous sporting event ever to take place at Vancouver's Empire Stadium, which was built specifically for the Games.

Landy led for most of the race but made a crucial runner's mistake coming around the last bend; he looked over his left shoulder to gauge Bannister's position. It briefly slowed him at the exact moment that Bannister was making his final push on the right, and the Brit shot past Landy and into the lead. Bannister finished the race in 3:58.8, not enough for the world record but 0.8 seconds ahead of Landy. Only three months after the first man had run a mile in under four minutes, two men had accomplished the feat in the same race. It was a thrilling and unforgettable moment in track and field history.

In 1967, Vancouver sculptor Jack Harmon commemorated the event by creating a bronze sculpture recreating the moment in which Bannister passed Landy. The sculpture still stands at the entrance of the Pacific National Exhibition fairgrounds. Upon seeing the sculpture for the first time, Landy famously quipped, "While Lot's wife was turned into a pillar of salt for looking back, I'm probably the only one ever turned into bronze for looking back."

Bathtub Racing

They say taking a shower is quicker than a bath, but they've obviously never attended Vancouver's annual Sea Festival, which features the locally invented sport of bathtub racing. Tubbers race from Nanaimo to Vancouver's Kitsilano Beach in bathtubs converted into boats and powered by gas engines. The race is held the last weekend of July every year.

The race began in Nanaimo in 1967, promoted by the city's mayor, Frank Ney. Ney was an odd man who clearly believed in the race, billed as the "Nanaimo to Vancouver Great International World Championship Bathtub Race." He would regularly dress as a pirate and tour the town and surrounding communities to raise awareness of the event.

There are other bathtub races around the world now, notably the Englefield Bathtub Derby in Auckland and the U.S.–Canadian Friendship race in Bremerton Washington, but Nanaimo's bathtub race remains the first and the most popular. Because of this, the Vancouver Island community has often been referred to as Tub City.

DID YOU  KNOW?

The term "cougar" is used to describe older women who seek to seduce younger men. It's often used in a derogatory sense, although free-spirited older women have recently sought to reclaim the label as a symbol of sexual empowerment. It also got a healthy boost from the ABC show *Cougar Town*.

Though the official etymology of the term is up for debate, most feel that the term originated in the Vancouver, and perhaps more specifically, the locker room of hockey's Vancouver Canucks, where players were warned to stay away from cougar-like women on the prowl.

Big Bill Werbeniuk

Are we all in agreement that snooker is a sport? No? Well, today it is, because it gives me an excuse to talk about one of Vancouver's most distinct athletic exports, snooker champion Bill Werbeniuk. Dubbed "Big Bill" in billiards circles for reasons you might have guessed (he was big, 136 kilograms big), Werbeniuk was a standout personality and folk hero on the pool circuit for much of the 1980s.

Did I mention he was big? Werbeniuk is famed for an instance during a televised World Championship match in which he struggled to reach across the table for a shot, only to split his pants. There was a loud ripping sound (often heard when trousers are torn), followed by a chorus of laughter from both the audience and Werbeniuk's opponent.

Lucky for Werbeniuk, he was generally a pretty relaxed man. He was messy, unkempt and always a little drunk, all of which can be attributed to the 30 to 40 pints of beer he drank per day. But he wasn't an alcoholic; it was medicinal. Big Bill suffered from tremors in his arms—a major problem for pool players— and his doctor suggested drinking to settle the shakes.

But Big Bill wasn't just a famous slob. He could really shoot. He once sank a red in the corner by causing the cue ball to jump in front of another ball, bounce over it, and knock the target into the pocket. The announcer called it "the pot of the century." At one time, Werbeniuk was the seventh-ranked snooker player in the world.

Werbeniuk's story has a sad ending. Late in his career, he began taking Propranolol to combat the effects on his heart because of his alcohol consumption, but the substance was banned as a performance-enhancer and Werbeniuk was subsequently banned from organized snooker. He played his last professional billiards match in 1990 and declared bankruptcy in 1991. He passed away in 2003 of heart failure. He was 56.

Lansdowne Racecourse Was a Bad Idea

In 1925, Lansdowne Track was opened in Richmond. Lansdowne hoped to compete with Hastings Racecourse as well as replace the local horse racetrack lost when Minoru Park was turned into an airstrip, but the facility had one major problem: location. Lansdowne was built over a peat bog that reared its ugly head at high tide. Occasionally, the ground became spongy, which made the horses run slower. The track was sold to Woodward's, the department store chain. Now it's the site of Lansdowne Centre, a shopping mall.

Mr. Baseball

Bob Brown loved baseball, but he wasn't much of a hitter and he knew it. Knowing that any manager who saw him play on a regular basis would cut him, he did the reasonable thing and found a team that he could manage himself. Of course, without experience, no owner would hire him to manage, so he knew he'd probably have to own the team, too. With that in mind, he came to the Pacific Northwest from Notre Dame when he was just 24, looking for a team he could buy cheaply. He found one in the Northwestern League's Vancouver Beavers and purchased the franchise for only $500 in 1910.

Sure enough, when baseball season started a few months later, Brown was the owner, manager and starting shortstop for the Beavers. He was living his dream. The team did well, too, turning a profit of $3500 in 1910 and winning the Northwestern League pennant in 1911. In 1912, Brown was offered $35,000 for the Beavers by a group in San Francisco.

He turned the offer down. Brown didn't just love baseball any-more; he loved Vancouver too, and he dedicated the rest of his life to growing the game in the city. When the Beavers' park was closed in 1913 so its owners could make room for warehouses, Brown bought the bleachers for $500, then went into the forest and built a brand new park on the south shore of False Creek with his bare hands (and some dynamite).

In 1913, Brown opened Athletic Park, which would be the home of Vancouver baseball for the next 38 years, producing international stars such as Cincinnati Reds pitcher Dutch Ruether, who would pitch a win in game one of the 1919 World Series.

Brown was a savvy marketer of the game, using all sorts of publicity stunts to draw people to the park. While Major League Baseball remained segregated, he staged a game versus the All-black All-Stars. He hosted the first night baseball game in Canada, a doubleheader. And he convinced Babe Ruth, Lou Gehrig and a host of other Hall of Famers to play an exhibition game in the pouring rain on October 19, 1934. Ruth went 0-for-2, hardly able to see the ball in the downpour. Gehrig played first base in galoshes while holding an umbrella. How very Vancouver.

Known as Mr. Baseball, Brown was inducted in the BC Sports Hall of Fame and later the Canadian Baseball Hall of Fame. He's been largely forgotten, even though his legacy lives on. Most baseball in Vancouver is now played at Nat Bailey Stadium, named for the man who launched White Spot, one of BC's largest restaurant chains. Bailey's first job was as a hot dog vendor in Bob Brown's Athletic Park.

Recreation and Culture

California has a beautiful coastline.
It can be a rough coastline. The waves are huge.
The rocks are steep. Same thing in Vancouver.
It has a beautiful coastline. It's dramatic.

–Jennifer Granholm, former U.S. Attorney General

SO MUCH TO DO

Vancouver is the only place in the world where you can golf, ski and kayak all on the same day. To that I'd say: make up your mind. If you're out to do all three in the daylight hours, you're probably not taking enough time to enjoy any one of them.

But the maxim remains true. Vancouver is the warmest non-island city in Canada, and its mild weather makes almost any activity a possibility on any given day.

With that much choice, it's no wonder that Vancouverites have often made some surprisingly odd choices when it comes to spending their leisure hours. Why swim in beautiful Kits pool, the largest saltwater pool in the world, when you could freeze your fanny off taking a dip in English Bay on New Year's Day? Why go for a leisurely hike through one of Stanley Park's beautiful nature trails when you could exhaust yourself trying to hike up the side of Grouse Mountain? Simply put: because that would be too easy.

It's not hard to enjoy yourself in Vancouver. But leave it to the locals to make it more difficult than it needs to be.

Polar Bear Swim

With multiple riots under their belts, it's probably safe to say that Vancouverites aren't always the most reasoned citizens, but few activities are crazier than the annual Polar Bear Swim held on New Year's Day. Each year, thousands of people strip down to their skivvies and dive headlong into English Bay, which is, as you may have guessed, freezing cold at that time of the year. The event has been an annual tradition since 1920, when six people observed the first small group of "polar bears" leaping into the bay. These days, as many as 10,000 people come out to observe the insanity.

The tradition was started by Peter Pantages, who owned a café on Granville Street for years. He loved to swim and vowed to do so every day of his life, which presented some challenges. However, the freezing water didn't deter him, and he organized the first swim as a unique holiday celebration.

But Pantages is not the most famous Polar Bear. That title belongs to Ivy Granstrom, who participated in her first polar bear swim in 1928. The blind 16-year-old must have enjoyed herself because she appeared at the next 77 consecutive swims.

The New Year's Day festivities have grown into a full-scale phenomenon. It's now an official event put on by the Vancouver Parks Board, and in any given winter, similar polar bear swims take place all over the continent.

If you're considering doing the swim, here are three helpful tips: bring something warm to wrap yourself in after the swim, bring something warm to drink afterwards and don't make the mistake of thinking that alcohol will take the edge off. Drinking alcohol does warm up your blood, but it will simply make the cold water feel even worse.

The Naked Swimmer

Annabelle Mundigel was a frequent participant in English Bay's Polar Bear Swim, but her biggest claim to fame was swimming from Vancouver to Bowen Island in 1938. She was the first person to do this, and she did it in quite the outfit. According to the *Province*, the 19-year-old was "clad in black trunks and a light woollen, apple-green singlet."

While this may have been appropriate attire for women at that time, it wasn't quite appropriate swimwear for the 27-kilometre trek, and Mundigel knew it. As soon as she was far enough out to avoid being seen, she stripped off her bathing suit, gave it to her family who was following in a boat and covered herself in lard. She did the swim in the nude, getting redressed just before coming into view of the small, cheering crowd on the island. She completed the swim in seven hours and 15 minutes.

DID YOU KNOW?

Coal Harbour was once exploding with fish. In 1882, Sprott's Oilery, a floating fish oil and cannery plant, set up shop on the water of Coal Harbour. At the time, the area was bursting with halibut, herring and octopus, and the plant made a killing in the area for about two years. What was their ingenious method? Throwing dynamite into the water. But the fish soon realized it was best to avoid the exploding harbour, and the company had to move on.

Seaside Pool

I'll be the first to admit that swimming in frigid waters doesn't sounds like a particularly enjoyable way to take a dip. Luckily, Kitsilano has plenty of nicer swimming holes. There are five outdoor pools in Vancouver, but the pool to end all pools (at least in

Canada) is Kits pool, located only a stone's throw away from beautiful Kitsilano beach.

Situated right on the shore, the outdoor pool's spectacular view of the ocean, the mountains and Vancouver's west skyline make it a must visit. It's Vancouver's only heated saltwater pool and, at 137 metres, it's the longest saltwater pool in Canada, almost three times longer than an Olympic-sized pool. There are three sections to it: a shallow area for families and small children, a middle area for exercisers and a deep end for more casual swimming.

All that said, why you'd want to swim in an artificial saltwater pool when the ocean is literally right beside you is beyond me.

The Grouse Grind

If you visit Vancouver and really want to remember your trip, try doing the aptly named grouse grind, which is indeed a grind and has been known to cause much grousing. The Grind, often described as "Mother Nature's Stairmaster," is a notoriously gruelling hike up Grouse Mountain.

The trail is unrelentingly steep, climbing 850 metres over three kilometres, with zero rest stops or flat stretches. The average grade is 17 degrees, with some stretches inclining up to 30 degrees. The average time of completion is approximately 90 minutes.

Although it sounds like a nightmare, the hike is a staggeringly popular one, with more than 100,000 people making the journey to the top of the mountain every year. In the summer, the trail is as oft-walked as Vancouver's main streets, frequented by everyone from casual hikers to serious athletes. The Vancouver Canucks even make each of their rookies and prospects do the grind as an initiation workout of sorts.

If you're looking to break any of the Grouse Grind's records, you'll find a number of Sebastians at the top of the list. The unofficial record time for completing the grind belongs to Sebastian Salas, who is said to have done it in under 24 minutes. The record for most grinds in 24 hours belongs to Sebastian Albrecht, who completed the hike a stunning 14 times between 6:30 AM and 11:00 PM on June 29, 2010. Why, we may never understand.

If you don't feel like lighting your quads on fire, you can take the gondola to the top, but prepared to have your breath taken away nonetheless: the staggering view, which overlooks the entire valley, has much the same effect as making the climb.

Don't make the common mistake of underestimating the hike. Vancouver's North Shore Rescue has conducted numerous rescues each year of hikers who collapse on their way up the mountain or begin too late in the day and find themselves lost in the dark.

One such individual to find herself lost on Grouse Mountain was *The X-Files'* Dana Scully, although it was part of a script: in a classic 1994 episode of the TV program, Scully is abducted by aliens in a scene that was filmed at the top of the mountain.

The Urban Peasant

One of Vancouver's most endearing television personalities was James Barber, the likable, simple food writer and cook with a slight limp and white beard who was known as *The Urban Peasant*. The show was broadcast and produced on Vancouver's CBC outlet, CBUT, and also aired in the United States on The Learning Channel.

The Urban Peasant set was built to resemble the actual kitchen in Barber's downtown Gastown loft, complete with a stove, sink, refrigerator, kitchen tables, plants, windows and a telephone. The set was so authentic that the phone would ring occasionally during the live-to-tape episodes, and what's more, Barber would answer it.

The conversations were usually brief, with Barber giving quick answers before hanging up and telling the viewers who had called. Sometimes it was supposedly a tradesman confirming an appointment. Sometimes it was his girlfriend. But come on—it was filmed in a television studio. Who was really calling?

As it turns out, the calls were from Barber's producer. The ringing phone was a clever way of reminding the cook when he'd forgotten an item in the oven or neglected to add a crucial ingredient to a dish.

Gung Haggis Fat Choy

If you needed further evidence that Vancouver is a diverse city, consider "Gung Haggis Fat Choy," an annual local event that combines Chinese New Year with the birthday of Scottish poet Robert Burns. The quirky celebration began in 1993, when Simon Fraser University student Todd Wong, a fifth-generation Chinese Canadian, was asked to help with the school's annual Robert Burns celebrations. As Wong learned about Scottish culture, he fell in love with it, and when he discovered that Burns' birthday fell only two days before Chinese New Year, he decided to celebrate the two cultures simultaneously.

He threw a private dinner for 16 friends, which he named Gung Haggis Fat Choy, a Scottish-ized version of the traditional Chinese New Year greeting, "Gung Hay Fat Choy," and adopted the persona, "Toddish McWong."

McWong's event has since taken off, spawning an annual festival put on by the university, TV features on France 3, ZDF German Public Television and the CBC as well as observation in places outside of Canada. The phenomenon even made its way to Scotland. In 2009, the 250th anniversary of Robert Burns' birthday, a travelling photo expedition of Gung Haggis Fat Choy saw its closing reception at Scottish Parliament, attended by McWong himself.

DID YOU KNOW?

Vancouverites eat out more than any other North Americans, which may be why a new restaurant opens up almost every week in the city. Of course, it might also be because Vancouverites are also notorious for tipping well.

Commitment to the Craft

The Got Craft fair is just super cool. Organized by Andrea and Robert Tucker, a husband and wife team who split their time between London, England, and Vancouver, the indie market features all sorts of neat, homemade stuff: plush toys, cookies, organic soaps, wooden jewelry, handbags made of recycled seatbelts and so on.

It takes place twice a year in both London and Vancouver, but no two fairs are like. Each event is juried to ensure that the quality of each vendor is top-notch and that the products on display are diverse and unique every year. And the limited swag bags, which include something from all the vendors at the fair, are worth camping out hours in advance for. Got Craft rocks.

Cycling's Critical Mass

Vancouver is heaven for cyclists for two big reasons. First, it's just a downright beautiful city—taking a morning bike ride along the Stanley Park seawall is one of the best ways to start a day. Second, it's often easier to get around the city by bicycle than by car—less traffic, more parking.

But in Vancouver, riding a bike is not just a convenient way to get around, it's also a common method of protest. Critical Mass, a bike movement launched in San Francisco in 1992, involves a large gathering of cyclists who travel in a bloc demonstrating the power of community and often protesting a current issue. Vancouver has adopted the movement in a big way.

Critical Mass rides happen on the last Friday of every month, with riders meeting at the Vancouver Art Gallery at 5:30 PM, rain or shine.

Critical Mass rides have become a popular community event— unless you drive. But it's hard to argue that the cyclists are blocking traffic when they *are* traffic.

Skating the Underground

Hidden beneath Hastings Street and just next to the freeway is Leeside, a fixture in Vancouver's skateboarding community. Originally built as part of a transit loop, Vancouver's policymakers forgot about it, and now the 49-metre-long tunnel is a skate park that is so underground that it's actually underground.

One entrance is obscured by trees and bushes. The other end is a dirt pathway that leads up the side of a hill. There's trash everywhere. But once you get inside, you'll find roughly a dozen handmade mini-ramps and grind poles.

Far from being a haven for reckless youth, Leeside takes its name from Lee Matasi, a 23-year-old skateboarder and artist who was killed in December 2003 for speaking out against gunplay. As he and a group of friends were leaving a club, one of them, Dennis White, fired a handgun into the air. When Matasi told White he was being unsafe, White fired back, literally, shooting Matasi in the chest and killing him instantly. The act was as senseless as it sounds.

The east side of the tunnel is the true Lee side. Not long after Matasi died, a local graffiti artist named Virus spray-painted a mural of the fallen young man on the tunnel wall.

The Write Track

Founded in 1988 and held every October, the Vancouver International Writers' Festival (VIWF) is one of the best literary festivals in Canada. That's not me talking, either. In 2010, it won an award for exactly that. The not-for-profit festival draws approximately 15,000 people over its six days, many of whom are the world's top writers. It's not rare to run into Margaret Atwood, Salman Rushdie, J.K. Rowling or the next big thing as you make your way through the crowd, nor is it rare to be read to by any of them.

Disasters

The day after the fire, I saw a burned-out hotel keeper selling whisky from a bottle on his hip pocket and a glass in his hand, his counter being a sack of potatoes.

–G.H. Keefer, city pioneer, commenting on
The Great Fire of 1886 in Vancouver

THE GREAT FIRE

The Vancouver you see today wouldn't be what it is if a fire hadn't burned the old one down. The Great Fire of 1886, Vancouver's largest disaster to date, razed the entire settlement just as it was getting started. Before the fire, as the population grew and more people moved into the area (none of whom brought a fire engine), the new citizens got careless and surrounded the city with highly flammable materials. Then they got even more careless and lit those materials on fire. It may not have been their finest hour.

There have been other incidents. A plane crash. A bridge collapse. But, in truth, Vancouver's next big disaster hasn't happened yet. A big earthquake is coming, and everybody knows it. But don't worry: this time around, Vancouver is prepared. They have a fire engine.

Terrible Forestry Practices

Vancouver is recognized as one of the most beautiful cities in the world, in large part because of its greenery. Few trees in the city can be cut down without a lengthy discussion or, at worst, public protest. Each chopped tree is the result of careful consideration.

The city didn't used to be so discerning, however. In the early days of the settlement, trees were toppled by the domino method. The lumberjacks would cut down large firs and cedars only, allowing the big trees to bring down the smaller trees as they fell into them. It was a particularly inelegant but quick way to go about this task, and left brushwood and timber strewn in every direction, sometimes to a depth of 3 metres.

Their method of clearing the brushwood was equally inelegant. Rather than safely removing the debris, the men simply lit the unwanted timber ablaze. Needless to say, it wasn't the brightest of ideas. The Great Vancouver Fire of 1886 was the result of a human-made brushfire that got out of control.

The Vancouver Fire

Early in 1886, Vancouver—then known as Granville but called Gastown by most—was selected as the western terminus for the cross-country line of the Canadian Pacific Railway. Needless to say, the economic return of the railway was substantial, as the city doubled in population from 1000 to 2000 and the provincial legislature gave the suddenly booming community the name it now holds. There was much optimism surrounding the city's future. There was also a bit too much brush.

With the rapid growth of the area and the lumber mills and vast fields of timber just south of the city, piles of felled trees and brush around the city grew steadily. Brushfires were occasionally reported, many set by entrepreneurs too lazy to clean up the mess like civic-minded people.

On Sunday, June 13, just after an unusually dry spring, high winds took ahold of one of these brushfires and dragged it toward the city. By the time the fire reached a shed on the south end, it was wildly out of control. Some witnesses said the fire was so hot that the buildings literally melted. The volunteer fire department, which had little else to fight the fire except a single manually drawn hose reel, chose instead to flee.

Most of the citizens rushed to Burrard Inlet, but the fire was so grand that it leapt across the inlet and consumed them on the other side. Many dived into the ocean and were rescued by a pair of lumberjacks who had built a raft out of criss-crossed logs. Fishermen drew people from the water as well, saving lives, although stories persist of some fishermen who beat desperate people from the sides of their boat with sticks.

The fire razed nearly every building in the community and took 40 lives. But the fire didn't dampen the hopes of the burgeoning community; instead, it inspired the citizens to be more wary of future fires. Additional brickwork was incorporated into the rebuild and a new fire engine was purchased from Ontario.

DID YOU KNOW?

Vancouver's first fire engine, a horse-drawn steam pump named the M.A. Maclean, arrived in Vancouver on August 1, 1886. The horses, however, arrived later, and for a time, the firefighters themselves had to pull the pump to fires. This was no easy feat: the steam pump weighed 5000 pounds (just over 2265 kilograms).

Fight Fire with Gunfire

While the fire in 1886 is a truly sad story, there's an excellent, smaller anecdote within it. Of the six homes that still stood after the fire, one belonged to a man who was seen perched atop his roof, surrounded by wet blankets, firing his revolver into the sky.

He staked his survival on the hope that the gunfire would create air flows that would direct the fire away from his house. While it remains one of the stupidest ideas in the history of Vancouver, it appears to have worked.

Hide in a Hole

Another better but still equally poor idea led to one death and two injuries as three men leapt into a hole left by the roots of a large overturned tree and covered themselves with dirt in hopes the fire would pass them by. The heat was too much for one of the men, known only as Bailey, and he vacated the hole in hopes of outrunning the fire. He made it only a few metres before dying.

The other two men in the hole thanked their lucky stars that they had chosen to stay put until a pouch of cartridges someone had been keeping in the hole exploded from the heat. Amazingly, they survived the whole ordeal.

The Whisky Survived!

There was little to celebrate after the Great Fire, but Jackson T. Abrey briefly took on local hero status in the aftermath of the inferno. As the survivors sat on the shore of Burrard Inlet wondering what just had happened to their settlement, they saw three barrels caught in the tide, floating out to sea. What was in them? While the settlers debated this question, Abrey leapt into his boat, rowed out to the barrels and retrieved all three.

When Abrey returned to shore, the citizens were delighted to find that the barrels were full of whisky. At that point, there were few who couldn't use a stiff drink.

OTHER BAD STUFF

The Collapse of the Second Narrows Bridge

In February 1956, construction began on Vancouver's Second Narrows Bridge, a six-lane, three-kilometre-long effort that would link Vancouver and North Vancouver across Burrard Inlet. (A word on the name: while the Second Narrows Bridge was designed as a replacement for an outdated drawbridge built in 1925, the new bridge was not christened the Second Narrows Bridge because the first was named the First Narrows Bridge. Rather, both bridges were actually named for their location: the second narrowing of Burrard Inlet.)

Before completion of the second Second Narrows Bridge, however, an accident occurred that necessitated the bridge taking on a new name. Unfortunately, that incident was a horrible bridge collapse.

On June 17, 1958, a little over two years after construction began and less than a year before the bridge was slated to be finished, the fourth and fifth spans of the Second Narrows Bridge tumbled into the ocean. The workers were putting the finishing touches on the fourth and had already begun work on the fifth, known as the anchor span, when suddenly a loud crack was heard. The anchor span trembled and sagged, then, within a matter of seconds, both spans—all 330 tonnes of them—collapsed into the water, along with scores of workers. Eighteen men were killed instantly or shortly thereafter. It was suspected that many of the workers were dragged under not by the weight of the fallen iron but by the weight of their toolbelts.

Two of the 18 men were the engineers said to be responsible for the collapse. The temporary arm they had designed to hold up the anchor span was cast as too slender, and it couldn't bear the force of the day's strong tide. A diver searching for bodies drowned as well—a man named Leonard Mott, who had done stunt diving for the film *20,000 Leagues Under the Sea*.

Four men also perished earlier in the construction process, which meant that the total number of workers who died during construction of the Second Narrows Bridge was 23. For that reason, the bridge was renamed the Ironworkers Memorial Second Narrows Crossing in 1994.

The Crash of Trans-Canada Airlines Flight 810

On December 9, 1956, Trans-Canada Airlines Flight 810 took off from the Vancouver International Airport. With reports of high winds, snow and other inclement weather along the route to Montréal, with stops in Calgary, Regina, Winnipeg and Toronto, the flight was delayed and airport officials briefly flirted with cancellation. When moderate weather began to prevail, however, the flight was cleared to go, and pilot Allen Clarke, known to many as "Granny Clarke" because he was cautious to a fault, took the plane and its 61 passengers and crew into the sky.

As the plane ascended, Clarke reported extreme turbulence, but clearance to continue climbing was granted. Then, only moments from breaking above the clouds, Clarke's instrument panel flashed —engine number two was on fire. He decided to turn the plane around. This is when the plane lost contact with Air Traffic Control.

Two hours later, a search for the missing flight officially began. Unfortunately, the same poor weather that had caused so many problems with Flight 810 made it impossible for the search and rescue pilots to see below them. Worse, by the time the planes could take to the sky, enough snow had fallen in the mountains to cover any visible wreckage. After 18 days, the search was called off.

Months later, a trio of hikers stumbled upon a piece of aluminum with code stencilled on it during a climb of Mount Slesse, 113 kilometres east of Vancouver. The code was quickly identified as coming from Flight 810's equipment.

Even with this solid lead, the search and rescue crew found the wreckage of Flight 810 by accident. Nothing was located until one of the climbers slipped down the eastern face of a sharp incline on one of BC's most daunting climbs and came across plane wreckage, baggage and human remains at the bottom. With this discovery, the searchers were able to find the collision point farther up the mountain.

Incredibly, the shape of Clarke's head and hat could be made out against the face of the mountain. It was instantly clear that nobody could have survived the crash. Had anybody been lucky enough to survive, they would have died in the sheer drop immediately following the impact.

Vancouver coroners attempted to extract the bodies, but the conditions were too dangerous to get even one body from the mass grave. As a result, to protect the sanctity of the site, the provincial government declared Mount Slesse a provincial cemetery.

Nanaimo Mine Disaster

On May 3, 1887, an explosion rocked the Vancouver Coal Mining and Land Company's top mine in Nanaimo, shaking the entire city and sending thick black smoke out from the mine where 155 of the town's men worked. Directly behind the plume of smoke was a cascade of towering flames that prevented anyone on either side from getting through.

It took 24 hours for the volunteer firefighting crew to extinguish the conflagration, at which point rescuers immediately rushed to the mine, desperate to find survivors. Near the entrance, they found that the top-of-the-line fan designed to send fresh air into the mine had melted, with the bodies of 13 men burned up along with it. The loss of the fan caused further problems in the rescue efforts, as the fresh air coursing through the veins of the mine had been replaced with a toxic gas. One rescuer later died from exposure to it.

After two days, the gas had cleared enough for the mine workers to enter the mine and for rescuers to continue their search. Seven men were found alive, many of whom were so dazed by the effects of the gas they couldn't remember how they had survived, nor what had even happened to endanger their lives in the first place.

No other survivors were found. Messages were etched in the timbers of the mine, several of them in Chinese, the nationality of many of the mine's workers. One message, written in English, read "Thirteen hours after explosion. In deepest misery. John Stevens." Another made little sense, stating, "One, two, three o'clock. William Bone. Five o'clock."

The cause of the tragedy was determined to be a planned explosion that had been set without the proper precautions, igniting with gas and coal dust. The explosion killed 148 of the 155 men, widowed 50 women and left 126 children without fathers. The families of the deceased men were permitted to remain on the land for free, with the Vancouver Coal Mining and Land Company and its community of workers pitching in to sustain them.

Earthquake City

Along with Seattle, Portland and much of Northern California, Vancouver lays within the Cascadia Subduction Zone, a major fault that could produce an earthquake of magnitude 9.0 or greater. The last earthquake on the fault took place before the settlers arrived in 1700, when a magnitude 9.2 earthquake occurred just off the coast of Vancouver Island, causing a tsunami that struck the coast of Japan.

Geologists have determined that great earthquakes occur along the Cascadia Subduction Zone once every 300 to 600 years, with the last one happening just over 300 years ago. So, if you're in the area, buy insurance.

And if you live in Richmond, buy a life jacket. During an earthquake, shaking can cause loosely packed, water-saturated sediments such as sand or silt to turn into a fluid mass—known as liquefaction. Because much of Richmond is built on a sand barge, scientists believe that, if the earthquake is strong enough, the liquefaction could cause some structures to slide right into the ocean.

Living in Coal Harbour, too, could pose problems. Most of the land now being developed was originally tidal flats that were filled in. It wouldn't be ideal to find yourself walking along the sidewalk in Coal Harbour when the big one comes, because the ground could turn to liquid beneath your feet.

DID YOU KNOW?

The largest quake in BC's recorded history was an 8.1 earthquake on August 21, 1949. Although it occurred just off the Queen Charlotte Islands, Vancouverites were lucky in that it occurred off the west side, primarily out to sea. Still, desperate to report some kind of local impact about the biggest quake modern British Columbia had ever seen, the *Province* ran a front page story about how it had stopped Mrs. Laurie Sanders' clock.

The March of the Feet

One of Vancouver's most recent unsolved mysteries has been the sudden trend of human feet washing up on its coast. A popular theory says that these occurrence are linked to a major disaster across the sea. Since August 2007, 12 running shoes—with detached feet inside—have been discovered on the banks of the Salish Sea. Two left feet have been matched with two right feet. Only four feet of three persons have been identified, and investigators have been unable to determine the gender of two of the 12.

Although all 12 feet were real, a number of hoaxes have been connected with the phenomenon. A foot discovered on June 18, 2008, turned out to be a skeletonized animal paw put in a sock and stuffed in a shoe. Several other running shoes washed up on Oak Beach, all of which were stuffed not with human feet, but with raw meat.

So what's going on with the feet? No one quite knows. Some have speculated that the feet belong to individuals who died in a boating or airplane accident, but no bodies have been discovered and no accidents have been reported. Others suspect foul play, although none of the feet show any signs of manual separation. One popular theory is that the bodies have been weighted down, but the feet have been separated as a result of natural decay.

One of the feet was identified as belonging to a man whose family reported that he had been depressed and they assumed he had committed suicide. This has led many investigators to believe that the feet aren't connected, no pun intended.

Another theory—perhaps the most intriguing—is that the feet belong to people who perished in the Asian tsunami on December 26, 2004. Though the feet have been difficult to examine because they had decomposed after so much time underwater, the forensic analysts were able to analyze the shoes. Many were produced in or before 2004, and some were only available in South Asia. Ocean currents and their ultimate northward tendencies up the Pacific Ocean could explain why the shoes have found their way from coast to coast.

The morbid enigma has fascinated many outside of Vancouver, with multiple national news reporting on each found foot. A handful of novels were written based on the phenomenon, and David Letterman once quizzed Canadian audience members during one of his programs about their involvement in the mystery.

Neighbourhoods

*I moved to Vancouver when I was 19 with the idea
that I would be there for six months to work on
a record. I immediately fell in love with it.*

–Sarah McLachlan, singer-songwriter

COMMUNITY STORIES

Vancouver is one of the most multicultural cities on earth. While the city doesn't have the wide cross-section of cities like Toronto or New York City, it boasts the largest population of foreign-born citizens. According to Statistics Canada, 35 percent of Vancouver's population of two million is foreign-born.

As a result, Vancouver is full of unique neighbourhoods and communities, some of which date back to the first days of the Hastings settlement itself.

Gastown

Vancouver's oldest district is Gastown, a section in the downtown core full of cobblestone streets, sidewalks and tourists stops. It's teeming with brickwork, the result of the city's decision to use brick when the original wood structures burned down during the Great Fire in 1886.

Still, much of Gastown's heritage is fake. The famous "steam" clock that blows at the corner of Water and Abbott is said to be a relic of the 1880s. But that is not true. Not only was the clock commissioned in 1977, but it's also powered by electricity. Much of the cobblestone was installed around the same time. The original streets were granite and the sidewalks were wood. In places where the asphalt has worn down, you can spot these street materials peeking through.

It Rains a Lot in Deep Cove

Few places in Vancouver are as beautiful as Deep Cove on
a sunny day. With the North Shore mountains behind it and the
water running through it, Deep Cove on a bright afternoon is
like something out of a poem. For those who love being outdoors,
the area is perfect for hiking, skiing, snowboarding and kayaking.

Of course, you'll need to put up with a little rain because you're
guaranteed to see some. The wet stuff falls in Deep Cove like
nowhere else in the Lower Mainland. The area receives an estimated
2200 millimetres of rain per year, 600 millimetres more than
downtown Vancouver.

DID YOU KNOW?

Author Malcolm Lowry, best known for his novel *Under the Volcano*, published in 1947, was one of Deep Cove's early residents. He wrote much of the classic's first draft in a cottage in the area in the late 1930s.

Underground Tunnels

Legend holds that downtown Vancouver is full of tunnels, most notably in Chinatown. These secret passageways were used for sneaking opium, smuggling goods and shuttling illegal immigrants. The evidence for these activities is seen while walking through the downtown area as you will likely come across suspicious, small squares of purple glass set in the sidewalk. The Chinatown tunnels were believed to be common knowledge in the early 1900s, with the police once taking a pickaxe to the sidewalk while the papers reported, "Getaway is underground" and "Police explore Chinese tunnels." But the tunnels are a myth. Beneath the purple glass are small rooms that merchants used to expand their premises. They're not connected to anything but the buildings above them. If you need to get around Chinatown, it'll have to be aboveground.

However, Vancouver does have underground passages, most of which are no longer in use. Among the best is the old CPR tunnel, originally designed for the train, but some parts of it are now used by the SkyTrain to bypass the Chinatown area. The tunnel's original entrance has been blocked off by a Costco. Another tunnel is the Bank of Canada tunnel that runs under West Hastings Street to safeguard against robberies, but it's practically never visited today.

In the early 1960s, Canada Post built a tunnel from the train station to their building at a cost of $1.6 million. It was used to bypass the downtown core while transferring the mail to the train, but it was deemed to be impractical only a few years later and closed down.

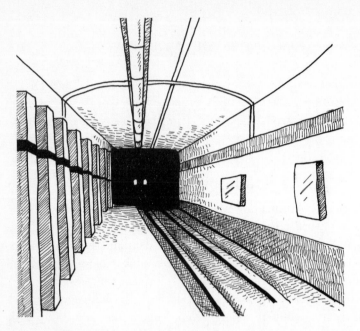

Now, the abandoned tunnel is used as a movie set—its dank and creepy atmosphere, complete with dripping water pipes and the rumbling of the nearby train station, makes it the location perfect for thrillers and adventure films.

Indian Arm

Getting mail to the citizens of Indian Arm during the early 1900s was an exceedingly difficult chore, especially because the tiny mining community is located on a 19-kilometre glacial fjord in North Vancouver that formed during the first Ice Age. The steep mountain slopes on either side of the city also made it impossible to build roads, so the only way in and out was by boat. As a result, for 30 years, the City of Vancouver was the proud owner of the only floating post office in the British empire, the Motor Vessel *Scenic*.

The Harbour Navigation Company purchased the boat in 1930 and redesigned it over the next two years for operation in shallow waters and so that her bow could pass over floats for easy unloading. By 1932, the Burrard Inlet Travelling Post Office was making regular stops.

Downtown Eastside

Vancouver's Downtown Eastside is often called the poorest postal code in Canada. Noted for its high incidence of drug use, prostitution, crime and violence, the area is widely regarded as one of the least inviting neighbourhoods in the nation, except to the unsavoury. Because Vancouver's climate is mild most of the year, the community attracts homeless from as far away as Toronto. Thousands wander the streets on any given day. The speed limit is 20 kilometres slower than in the rest of the city, simply because transients can wander out in front of your vehicle at a moment's notice.

In 2003, the City of Vancouver opened Insite, North America's first legal supervised injection facility where addicts could receive clean drugs and needles, health care and addiction counselling treatment, if they wanted. Because the Downtown Eastside has one of the highest rates of HIV in the country, using unsterilized needles to inject can often be a death sentence. Insite operates on a harm-reduction model, simply trying to mitigate the danger many of the Downtown Eastside's residents find themselves in every day.

DID YOU  KNOW?

The term "skid row," used to describe the seedy area of any given city, originated in Vancouver in the 1800s. Vancouver's skid row is the Downtown Eastside on Hastings Street, which used to be the site of wooden skids constructed so that logs could be dumped into Burrard Inlet and floated to the lumber mill. The term stuck, and when Vancouver's most unseemly citizens began to make the place home, it morphed into a term for seedy areas in general.

Strathcona

Located just west of Chinatown and even including some parts of it, Strathcona is Vancouver's oldest residential community. Built up around the Hastings Mill Store in the 1880s, Strathcona has a rich historic and architectural heritage, as well as reasonably priced real estate. Why's that? Because Strathcona is right next to the Downtown Eastside, which has many shady characters.

Strathcona is incredibly multicultural. Sixty-one percent of the residents report Chinese to be their first language, but only 24 percent of the remaining 39 percent report their first language to be English. It's a very diverse community.

Vancouver has had an interesting relationship with Strathcona. Many Vancouverites simply find all the houses unsightly and have mounted campaigns to demolish the entire area and put up apartment buildings and a freeway connector. Between 1959 and 1965, nine blocks of the neighbourhood were torn down, and residents feared the gentrification process would wipe out the entire area. They formed SPOTA (Strathcona Property Owners and Tenants Association), launched fund-raising campaigns and appealed to politicians. Luckily, the pleas caught a sympathetic ear in Paul Hellyer, the federal minister of housing. He put a quick stop to the community's problems by freezing the federal funds for urban renewal.

DID YOU  KNOW?

Alexander Road, unofficially known as "Food Street," contains more than 50 Asian restaurants within two blocks.

Island Getaways for the Rich and Famous

Sick of having neighbours? Tired of buying boring old houses? Why not swing for the fences? The coast of British Columbia is a great place to find a wicked deal on a private island.

Canada has the largest number of islands of any country in the world, and BC currently has more for sale than any other province. The prices aren't too shabby either. Although some islands aren't changing hands without an offer in the tens of millions, the smaller islands are listed at no more than $30,000.

Of course, you'll have to spring for a few accessories, such as a boat or seaplane, and you'll probably want to build a house as well. But if you're in the market for an island, I can only assume that you're not overly worried about the additional costs.

DID YOU KNOW?

Comedian Robin Williams owns a patch of floating real estate off the Sunshine Coast.

Asia West

If you're in Richmond and in the mood for a disorienting cultural experience, you could stop by the curious shopping district dubbed Asia West. The strip sprung up in the late 1990s, after Hong Kong was repatriated to China and the Richmond area saw a major spike in Asian immigration.

Asia West is not simply a strip of Chinese stores—it's *so* Asian that it will blow your mind. All the signs, music and announcements are in Cantonese, Mandarin, Korean and Japanese. The fashions are unique and eye-popping, and the decorative and housewares sections are unlike anything you'll find at Zellers. The area features Chinese herbalists, Japanese housewares, designer luggage and plenty of fashion-forward clothes and shoes for petite women. There are also huge Asian supermarkets such as the T&T, where you can select a fish from the tanks, which the staff will deep-fry for you while you shop.

CHINATOWN

The Vancouver Ghetto

Vancouver's Chinatown, the largest Chinese community in Canada, is so close to the downtown core that you'd be forgiven for assuming the two communities grew up side-by-side, all friendly-like. Of course, that assumption couldn't be further from the truth. In the early 1900s, Chinatown was Vancouver's ghetto, and white settlers who lived nearby looked upon the area with scorn.

Early Chinatown was notorious not just for its opium dens but for its brazen opium growth. Raw opium was cultured in Chinatown and carried through the city in baskets. Rumours of all sorts of debauchery going on beneath the city circulated as well. Many spoke of Chinatown's secret tunnels of villainy.

Laws were passed to discourage white citizens from venturing into Chinatown. One such law allowed the city to revoke Chinese business licences if they hired white workers, and when the Hongkong Cafe turned its nose up at the rule, the city closed it down until the white waitresses were fired. In explaining these strong-arm tactics, W.W. Foster, the chief of police at the time, said, "In view of the conditions under which the girls are expected to work, it is almost impossible for them to be so employed without falling victim to some sort of immoral life." Numerous attempts were also made to simply run the Chinese population out of the city.

Chinese Riot of 1887

The Chinese Riot of 1887 is poorly named, primarily because Vancouver's early Chinese citizens were the target of the riot and not the instigators. After the Canadian Pacific Railway was completed in Vancouver, many of the Chinese workers remained in the settlement and joined the logging force. However, the whites of the area didn't quite care for this, feeling the Chinese were creating too much competition for work and getting too comfortable. In February, they decided to run the Asian population out of town.

Near midnight, a mob of nearly 300 men, lanterns in hand, ambushed the Chinese workers in their tents. They flipped tents, kicked the workers who didn't run and chased those who did run through the snow and over the edge of a cliff.

Apparently a good night's sleep didn't satisfy the mob, who moved into Chinatown the following morning to cause more damage. They rounded up 100 of the area's Chinese residents, forced them onto a boat and sent to the boat to Victoria, to the cheers of a crowd of nearly 600 men.

The riot resulted in one of the rare early cases where the provincial government sided with the Asian population and ordered that the Chinese citizens be allowed to return to Vancouver. Vancouver's charter was revoked, and when the citizens drafted a letter of protest and threatened more violence if the Chinese were sent back, three dozen police constables were assigned to accompany them from Victoria to calm the out-of-control mob.

Asiatic Exclusion League

In May 1905, the Asiatic Exclusion League (AEL), a racist organization aimed at preventing East Asian immigration, was formed in San Francisco by 67 labour unions. The league saw immediate success (if you can call it that), lobbying to segregate Asian school children in the area.

Shortly thereafter, on August 12, 1907, a sister organization with the same name was formed in Vancouver with many of the same intentions. The group's stated aim was to keep Oriental immigrants out of British Columbia.

Fortunately, the Vancouver branch of the AEL wasn't quite as effective as its forerunner in San Francisco. Unfortunately, it's largely because the league resorted to violence almost right away. Less than a month after the AEL was established, a series of incendiary speeches at City Hall inspired thousands to march into Chinatown in protest of the growing community. Initially, the crowd was simply shouting racist slogans, but it didn't take long for the situation to escalate. As the mob paraded through the streets, they vandalized buildings, causing thousands of dollars worth of damage.

Next, the angry horde moved to Japantown, whose citizens were a little more prepared, fighting back the crowd armed with clubs and bottles.

After the riots, interest in the AEL began to die down (perhaps with all that aggression released), but the group was a little more successful their second time around. The organization resurfaced in the early 1920s, successfully lobbying for the passage of the Chinese Immigration Act of 1923, which ended virtually all Chinese immigration to Canada.

Komagata Maru

The *Komagata Maru* was a Japanese steamship that sailed from Hong Kong to Shanghai to Yokohama and then to Vancouver, carrying 376 hopeful Indian immigrants. The boat arrived in Burrard Inlet on May 23, 1914, only to be met with hostility and racism.

Although the Indian passengers had committed an illegal immigration act, they felt that, as British subjects, they would be allowed to settle in Canada once they arrived. However, the Canadian government responded to burgeoning anti-Asiatic sentiment in the area and prohibited disembarkation from the ship. Until mid-July, the passengers were trapped aboard the boat, which was hardly a cruise ship, as debate raged over what to do with them. In the meantime, Vancouverites staged demonstrations on the shore in protest of the "raghead invasion," and a gunboat was anchored nearby to prevent the passengers from trying to escape the ship.

In the end, only the 20 passengers were admitted to Canada, and on July 23, the ship was forced to return to Asia. When the ship arrived in India, police tried to arrest Gurdit Singh Sandhu and the other men it believed responsible for the illegal journey, which kicked off a fearsome struggle in which 19 of the passengers were killed, others were wounded and most were arrested and confined all through World War I. Sandhu managed to escape and lived in hiding for nearly a decade, until Mahatma Gandhi convinced him to give himself up as a true Indian patriot and hero. When he did, he was imprisoned for five years.

DID YOU KNOW?

The immigration officer who first met the *Komagata Maru* when it sailed into the Vancouver port was "Cyclone" Taylor, the hockey player that had led Vancouver to a Stanley Cup in 1915, one year later. As part of his contract with the Ottawa Senators in 1907, Taylor was promised a job with the Canadian Immigration Branch, and he kept the job when he signed with the Vancouver Millionaires in 1912.

Woon Fon Sing

On July 26, 1924, at the height of anti-Asiatic sentiment in Vancouver, a nanny named Janet "Nursie" Smith was found dead on the floor of her employer's basement laundry room with a gunshot wound in her temple. The only other person in the home at the time Woon Fon Sing, the Asian houseboy who found her body, and his nationality stood as the primary piece of evidence that he was guilty of homicide.

Fon Sing insisted he was innocent of the crime, and since no real evidence linked him to the death, the police were unable to arrest him. Instead, they simply kidnapped him, holding him overnight and trying to threaten and beat a confession from him. It didn't work. Shortly after he was released, Sing was once again kidnapped, this time held for six weeks by the KKK, and shortly after his captors let him go, he was formally arrested for the crime. He never stood trial however; a second investigation into the murder ruled that Nursie had shot herself. Woon Fon Sing was released. He returned to China in 1926.

Japantown

In the early 1900s, Chinatown was neighbour to Japantown, a small community of Japanese immigrants, full of shops, house, and markets. The residents were active and generous in helping other Japanese settle throughout the province. By the 1930s, the neighbourhood had developed a strong commercial core, with its own department store, and even its own championship baseball team, the Asahi. So why is Chinatown still a major part of the city's downtown structure and Japantown a distant memory?

The answer is Pearl Harbor. On December 7, 1941, the Japanese attack on the U.S. Naval base in Honolulu prompted the Canadian federal government to order the removal of all Japanese Canadians living within 100 miles (160 kilometres) of the Pacific Coast. BC politicians had long been looking for an excuse to remove the Asian communities, and the war was just the excuse to erase Japantown from Vancouver.

In 1943, the Canadian government gave permission for the seized land to be sold off, and when the ban was lifted and the Japanese were allowed to return to the coast in 1949, most had nothing to return to and went elsewhere.

City Treasures

Vancouver can dress up and act quite sophisticated when she wants to. But she'd rather put on her woollies and galoshes and go splash in a puddle.

–David Lansing, travel writer

COOL STUFF

Vancouver has so much cool stuff that much of it is simply tucked away, just waiting for someone to take it out and play with it. The Coaster. The Challenger Relief Map. The Nine O'Clock Gun. The wreckage of the Beaver. Okay, maybe the bottom of the ocean isn't storage. And you probably shouldn't play with cannons. But still.

Everywhere you turn in Vancouver, it seems you'll come across an artifact from the city's past with a story to tell or see a statue erected in honour of a great man whose tale is not told often enough. If you run out of stories to hear or to tell in Vancouver, it's possible you wandered too far out of town. Go back. Vancouver's history is littered with lost and found treasures, small trinkets and big toys.

The Coaster

In 1948, Vancouver's beloved wooden coaster, The Giant Dipper, was torn down to make way for Hastings Racecourse, much to the chagrin of those who thought old roller coasters were a much more enjoyable ride than horses (count me among them). Thankfully, Vancouver didn't have to wait long to get another wooden coaster. Ten years later, the city said hello to The Coaster, at the time the largest wooden roller coaster in Canada.

The Coaster was built board by board in 1958 and has been entertaining and terrifying people as a mainstay of Playland Amusement Park ever since. It's no wonder. If you aren't scared by the speeds The Coaster can reach—72 kilometres per hour—then the fact that the rickety old structure feels on the verge of coming apart under your feet usually does the trick. Now the oldest operating roller coaster in Canada, The Coaster has been named a roller coaster landmark by the American Coaster Enthusiasts organization and is widely held to be one of the 10 best roller coasters in the world.

The Challenger Relief Map

One of BC's coolest treasures is the massive relief map of south-western British Columbia created by George Challenger and his family over a seven-year period. The map, which gives an incredible view of BC's geography and terrain, occupies 6080 square feet. Constructed from nearly one million pieces (989,842, to be exact) of quarter-inch fir plywood, the map was painted and assembled on 1.1 × 2.7-metre plywood panels. It's not a boring old two-dimensional map either. The Challenger Relief Map's vertical scale, exaggerated six times, is one inch to 304 metres. The *Guinness Book of Records* cites the map as the largest of its kind in the world, a cartographical masterpiece.

Challenger, who arguably covered more ground in BC than anyone as a prospector, miner, survey crewman and sawmill operator, took up map-making in the 1920s, largely as an aid to his work. He fell in love with the practice. During World War II, he created a map for military purposes, and he started on the BC relief map in 1946, hoping to share his love of the province with others.

In 1954, the BC Pavilion at the Pacific National Exhibition was built to house the map, and Challenger was so proud of it that he asked for his ashes to be kept in an urn beneath it after his death. When he passed away in 1964, that's what was done.

In 1997, however, the BC Pavilion was torn down, Challenger's ashes were returned to his family, and the map has been in a storage warehouse in Richmond ever since. A section of it was put on display during the Vancouver Olympics in 2010, but the map awaits a permanent home. The fact that this incredible achievement is collecting mothballs in the industrial district seems like a downright travesty.

Burnaby Centennial Parker Carousel

Carousels are a dying form of entertainment. As many as 6000 were once in operation in North America, but nowadays there are fewer than 250. One of the best carousels is the 100-year-old "Parker #119" at Vancouver's Burnaby Village Museum. The machine earned this name because it's the 119th such carousel made by the great C.W. Parker, whose company built approximately 1000 carousels in the early 1900s. Parker #119 toured Texas in 1913, where its 41 horses were a hit, and after two years, the ride was shipped back to the carousel company's factory in Kansas to wait for a permanent buyer.

The Happyland Amusement Park in Vancouver purchased the carousel in 1936, and it remained there until the park closed in 1957. For the next 30 years, it was brought out for the summer, left in the rain, then put away once the weather turned.

In 1989, when it was announced that the carousel was to be sold off, horse by horse, at an auction in New York City, the Burnaby Village Museum stepped up, launching a movement to restore and keep the machine. The coolest part about this project is that the museum raised $350,000 by soliciting sponsors who were given the privilege of naming the horses. Unsurprisingly, one horse, a palomino jumper, was named Mr. Ed.

The Nine O'Clock Gun

Stanley Park is home to all sorts of interesting treasures, but one of the most well-known is the Nine O'Clock Gun, a 5-kilogram muzzle-loaded naval cannon. The gun is nearly 200 years old, having been cast in Woolwich, England, in 1816. Seventy-eight years later, the Department of Marine and Fisheries in BC brought the cannon to Stanley Park to keep fishermen abreast of the time. It was to be fired at 8:00 AM, noon, 1:00 PM and the close of fishing at 6:00 PM. Prior to the installation of the cannon, the Brock Point Lighthouse keeper signalled the time by detonating a stick of dynamite at the shore.

Few know that the cannon, which is famed for firing only at 9:00 PM, actually discharged for the first time on October 15, 1898, by Captain W.D. "Davey" Jones…at noon. The 9:00 PM firing was established later as a time signal for the general population, as well as a way to allow the chronometers of ships in the port to be accurately set.

Even now, the gun remains a ritual by which you can set your watch.

The cannon has missed a few days of work, however, usually because mischievous students at the nearby University of British Columbia have stolen or vandalized it. In 1969, the students stole it and held it for "ransom" on behalf of the BC Children's Hospital. After it was returned, the cannon was surrounded by a stone and metal enclosure to prevent further hostage situations.

DID YOU KNOW?

Curiously, Captain W.D. Jones died on March 1, 1928, at exactly 9:00 PM.

Classical Chinese Garden

The first full-size Chinese garden built outside of China, the Dr. Sun Yat-Sen, was completed just in time for Expo '86 and is a tribute to the Chinese gardening tradition of the Ming Dynasty. The garden, which features asymmetrical arrangements of rocks and plants, serpentine pathways and a breathtakingly still pond, is one of the most beautiful places in the city.

As well as a tribute to the ancient dynasty, it's also a fully authentic representation of a classical Chinese garden, because Vancouver's climate is mild enough to support many of the same plant varieties as the Chinese gardens after which Dr. Sun Yat-Sen modelled it.

The Ben Franklin Submarine

Sitting outside the Vancouver Maritime Museum on Kits Point is the *Ben Franklin*, one of the world's greatest deep-sea submarines. Built by Swiss inventor Jacques Picard (the man for whom *Star Trek* captain Jean-Luc Picard was named), the 130-ton ship has four external electric propulsion pods that are powered by lead batteries stored outside the hull. The submarine boasts a whopping 29 observation portholes and is capable of plunging to depths of 914 metres. It was a marvel of deep-sea exploration in the late 1960s.

Unfortunately, nobody was overly interested in deep-sea exploration at that time, especially when scientists were busy exploring the moon. *Ben Franklin*'s maiden voyage, which took place in the summer of 1969, was dwarfed by the first moon landing (and Bryan Adams getting his first six-string). When the *Ben Franklin* emerged from the ocean on August 14, it was to little fanfare and a place in the back pages of the local newspaper.

But the *Ben Franklin* continued to make history. One of its next dives was the first deep-sea experience of Dr. Robert Ballard, who later discovered the wreck of the *Titanic*.

Ben Franklin ran aground on a reef in 1971 and was sold soon after to Vancouver businessman John Horton, who had plans for the submarine but simply wound up leaving it in a Vancouver shipyard for nearly three decades. In December 1999, *Ben Franklin* was given to the Vancouver Maritime Museum, who refurbished the submarine and placed the triumph of deep-sea exploration out front.

The Shipwrecked *Beaver*

Fans of the Prospect Point lighthouse can thank the *Beaver*, a steamship that slammed into the point on July 26, 1888, and ran aground on the rocks. She sat there for four years, picked over by souvenir hunters and scavengers, before the wake of another steamer pushed her off the rocks and allowed her to sink with some dignity.

The wreck was an unfortunate end for the *Beaver*, which was the first steamship on the West Coast when it was built in 1835 and had been in service both to the Hudson's Bay Company and the Royal Navy for over 50 years. In colonial days, the boat helped immeasurably in spreading British influence, carrying James Douglas to Vancouver Island to build Fort Victoria and carrying him to Fort Langley 13 years later.

Deservedly, some parts of the ship ended up in Vancouver Museum, which houses the anchor, both paddlewheels and a handful of items people fashioned from the ship's wood. But most of the *Beaver* is still sitting at the bottom of First Narrows Inlet.

In October 1888, three months after the accident, Vancouverites put up a lighthouse at Prospect Point to prevent further shipwrecks. It was replaced with the current Prospect Point lighthouse in 1948.

Granville Street Neon

Neon signs are a staple of the Las Vegas Strip, but many don't realize that over a brief period in the 1940s and 1950s, Vancouver was actually the neon capital of the Western Hemisphere. In the 1920s, Neon Products, a Vancouver-based outdoor advertising company, obtained a patent for neon signs that saw them become one of the largest sign companies in the world. With one of the biggest distributors of the neon in their own backyard, Vancouver developed an unhealthy obsession with neon. By 1953, the city was said to have had over 18,000 neon signs. Only Shanghai had more at that time.

If you really wanted an all-you-can-eat visual buffet of neon, the place to be was Granville Street, which had so much neon signs that the strip was dubbed "The Great White Way." This was an endearing term at first, but it soon became a derogatory one. As the city grew, the gaudy inner city lights were considered an eyesore, especially in contrast to Vancouver's natural beauty, and in the 1960s, anti-neon legislation was introduced to get rid of all the signs.

Of course, shortly after the legislation was introduced, people began bemoaning the dying downtown, and neon has been working on a revival ever since. These days, there's quite a bit of neon on Granville Street, albeit not as much as there used to be.

The BowMac Sign

If you've ever driven along Broadway, you've likely noticed the massive BowMac sign, which is the largest commercial sign in Vancouver. It was the brainchild of Vancouver billionaire Jim Pattison. In 1957, Pattison was the general manager of the Bowman Maclean automobile dealership, which was struggling to get one up on the auto dealers on either side of it: Black Motors to the east and Dueck's to the west. Pattison's bright idea was to erect a massive, vertical neon sign that couldn't be missed.

The sign is 30 metres tall, with enough cement at its base to pave 40 residential driveways. It has 16 kilometres of wiring and can be seen, appropriately, from 16 kilometres away. When the sign debuted in 1959, it went into the *Guinness Book of Records* as the world's largest free-standing neon sign.

BowMac is no longer in business, and a Toys "R" Us now occupies the space. But the city didn't want to lose a part of its heritage, so the vertical Toys "R" Us sign is simply laid over one side of the BowMac sign, a unique way of simultaneously acknowledging the past and the present.

Warren Harding Memorial

Many of the beautiful memorials in Vancouver were created by Italian sculptor and art teacher Charles Marega, who moved to Vancouver with his wife in 1938. Marega has been called the greatest sculptor in Western Canada, and his work is all over the city of Vancouver. The two lions at the south approach to Lion's Gate Bridge and the David Oppenheimer bust in Stanley Park belongs to him. The fountain across from English Bay, which commemorates Old Black Joe, the lifeguard, is Marega's handi-work as well. But if there's a Marega creation that stands out as unusual, it's the Warren Harding Memorial in Stanley Park.

What did the 29th president of the United States do to earn a statue in Vancouver? In July 1923, Harding became the first American president to visit Canada, giving a speech at Stanley Park and apparently wowing the crowd of 50,000 with his personable nature and oration skills. Somewhat smitten, the Canadians wished him the best as he continued his journey north to Alaska. Seven days later, the 57-year-old died suddenly of a heart attack in San Francisco upon his return from the trip north. Vancouverites were devastated by the news. The local Kiwanis Club immediately decided to initiate an international competition for a suitable monument to honour the fallen president, and Marega was declared the victor.

DID YOU  KNOW?

Although Warren Harding may have been the first president to visit Vancouver, he wasn't the first to make history in the city. In 1865, Vancouver received its first ever telegraph. It told of the assassination of Abraham Lincoln at the hands of John Wilkes Booth.

Lord Stanley Statue

At the entrance to Stanley Park is a statue of Frederick Arthur Stanley, the sixth Governor General of Canada and the man for whom the park is named, but the story behind how it came to be built is an interesting one.

Sometime in 1950, J.S. Matthews, the city archivist, stumbled across a letter that had been written on October 19, 1889, promising Lord Stanley a statue. Matthews couldn't determine who had written the letter, but he knew the promise had never been kept, so he launched a fund-raising campaign to get the statue erected immediately. Ten years later, the money was finally raised and the statue was erected.

The Dark Side

*I never did smoke that much pot;
never was a big pothead.*

–Tommy Chong, comedian and actor

SEX AND DRUGS

Do you like sex? Do you like drugs? If you answered yes to one or both of these questions, there's a good chance you might be from Vancouver. Or that you should go there right away.

Vancouver may be well known for its terrific skyline, amenable climate and beautiful geography to some. But to a whole different clientele, the city is renowned around the world for its women, who have inhabited some of the most popular brothels and strip clubs on North America's west coast, and its weed, which many consider to be the finest on the continent. It may not be Sin City, but it's a city that's never minded a little sin now and then. If you want to spend the weekend naked and high, there's someone in the area code who likes the way you think. And they're probably at Wreck Beach.

Stoner Vancouver

Shortly after Vancouver-born Ross Rebagliati won the first-ever Olympic gold in the sport of snowboarding in 1998, he was stripped of the medal for failing a drug test that revealed him as an enjoyer of that famous "BC Bud."

Because marijuana was not on the International Olympic Committee's official list of banned substances, Rebagliati was given back his medal, but the public incident drew attention to Vancouver's seedy pot culture, which is a major contributor to the city's mellow vibe.

While dedicated stoners could have told you BC was the place to get high before, the popularity of local herb exploded after this incident. Pot tourism has flourished ever since, with many calling the city "Vansterdam." If weed is your bag, there are many, many places to stop in Vancouver, the most important of which is the pot district on West Hastings, a block of pot hotspots and pot paraphernalia stores, beginning at the Dominion Building and ending at the Blunt Bros. pot cafe. Be sure to check out the second floor of these buildings as well, because you might catch a glimpse of the little signs advertising pot seeds, if you're brazen enough to try growing your own. For the record, the police see these signs too, but they've got plenty of other things to do besides arresting seed sellers.

BC bud is widely held to be some of the best in the world, with a Vancouver Island strain called Hydra recently taking second place in the 24th annual High Times Cannabis Cup, a pot breeders' competition in Amsterdam.

If you're unfamiliar with some of the common strains of Vancouver marijuana, here's a quick rundown of a few you might expect to find: Blue Truck, Willie's Wonder, Crystal Globe, Great White Shark (which is actually red), Purple Pineberry, Hemp Star, Grape Punch, Sweet Skunk, Champagne (for bikers only) and Kush, the rare strain many pot connoisseurs claim is the best bud around.

Cheech and Chong

There are few more enduring icons of stoner culture than Cheech Marin and Tommy Chong, the pothead pair whose stand-up comedy routines earned them a major audience in the 1970s and 1980s. Unsurprisingly, considering Vancouver's deep-seated ties to pot, the pair got their start in Vancouver.

While neither Cheech nor Chong are from Vancouver, Chong had moved to the city in the 1950s, originally as a musician, but soon shifted into comedy. He took over the Shanghai Junk strip club and turned it into a strip club that occasionally featured improv comedy. Or a comedy club that occasionally featured stripping. Whatever. People came in.

Cheech came to Vancouver in the late '60s after dropping out of California State University to avoid the draft and wound up working in the city for nine months, making music and acting in an improv comedy troupe called City Works.

He met Chong, the two of them honed an act, and within a year, they returned to Los Angeles to bring the act to a bigger stage.

Even as Cheech and Chong became international stars, references to Vancouver remained a large part of their act—the cop who's always trying to bust them is based on a member of the Vancouver Police.

Wreck Beach

Located in Pacific Spirit Regional Park on Vancouver's West End is Wreck Beach, the city's most popular destination for those who believe life should be clothing-optional. It's a hive of unclothed activity, with board games, beach sports, live music, casual drug use and philosophical discussions. The only hobby forbidden is photography, for good reason.

An episode of *Lifestyles of the Rich and Famous* once deemed the peculiar hotspot as one of the world's 10 most exclusive places, and not because it's difficult to fit in at the beach. It's actually quite easy. Rather, the "exclusiveness" has to do with getting to the beach. In order to participate in the nude revelry, you have to climb down a steep, cliffside staircase at the University of British Columbia. One imagines it's out-of-the-way-ness is a large part of why Vancouver's police ignore the brazen flouting of the public indecency laws. Or maybe people simply have a lot of fun there.

The story behind Wreck Beach's name is almost as interesting as what goes on down on the sand. The tale dates back to 1928, when three log barges and a floating grain container were intentionally sunk off the beach's shores by the Pacific Tug and Barge Company in order to create a breakwater for a large log storage ground. The name was unofficial until 1982, when UBC students lobbied for the change from University Beach, no doubt because a nude beach deserves better than such a bland name.

DID YOU KNOW?

The Vancouver sex shop Art of Loving got into hot water when the owners announced plans to put on a theatrical performance that featured an unsimulated act of oral sex. The police intervened, no doubt because public sexuality is against the law, but when the store pointed out that they could just film the performance and sell the tape to their patrons, the cops relented and the event took place. It was quite well attended.

The Penthouse Cabaret

Even if you're not the type to set foot inside its walls, you have to admire the plucky determination of the Penthouse Cabaret, one of Vancouver's premier strip clubs. Its sleazy interior, pervading sense of history and famous neon sign has made the place a cult icon—maybe even a landmark.

The Penthouse, located in the downtown core along Seymour Street, has been home to shady dealings ever since it opened in 1947. In the old days, it operated as an unlicensed, after-hours "bottle club" where people drank illegally. Police frequently raided the club, most notably in its first year of business, when 49 bottles of hard liquor and 467 bottles of beer were seized in what the *Vancouver Sun* called "the largest liquor seizure of the decade." The owners were charged with selling liquor, but the charges were later thrown out.

Still, it must have spooked them somewhat as the Penthouse got a licence in the 1950s to operate as a cabaret. Granted, the club was without a liquor licence, so the drinking remained illegal. The Penthouse used lookouts and buzzers and sly messages to get customers to hide their booze at their feet or in secret drawers when the police came in, which could be as often as three times a week.

The club became a favourite hangout for celebrities in town to play other clubs. Frank Sinatra, Bing Crosby, Bob Hope, Gary Cooper, Louis Armstrong, Frankie Laine and Harry Belafonte were among the big names to kick back at the Penthouse. Sammy Davis even lived at the club for a month.

A couple years ago, the owners found a stash of signed photos of Louis Armstrong, Joe Frazier and Sammy Davis Jr. hidden in a hole in the wall.

The club finally got a liquor licence in 1965, right around the time it brought in go-go dancers. It was also rather conveniently full of hookers on any given night around this time, and its owners were arrested again in the early '70s for running a brothel. In the 1980s, it officially became a strip club, and now operates as a sometimes strip club, sometimes music venue, sometimes locations for films and photo shoots.

Joe Philliponi, one of the Penthouse Cabaret's original owners, was killed during a robbery attempt in 1983.

Playmates

Pamela Anderson may be the most famous Playboy playmate to come out of Vancouver, but she wasn't the first and she certainly won't be the last. Ken Honey, a *Playboy* photographer and scout, of sorts, finds Vancouver a delightful place to meet women willing to appear in his employer's magazine, minus their clothes. He discovered Heidi Sorenson, *Playboy*'s July 1981 Playmate of the Month, at a bikini contest sponsored by Vancouver's CFUN radio. Honey discovered a bevy of other Playboy playmates on his trips to Vancouver as well, such as Kelly Tough and Dorothy Stratten. Finding Vancouver's gene pool to their liking, Playboy opened up a branch in Vancouver and continues to hold Playboy scouting nights at local watering hole, *Au Bar*.

No. 5 Orange

A strip club with a little less history but a few pretty good stories is the No. 5 Orange, a grimy little dive in Vancouver's downtown Eastside that's played host to a number of famous people. Prior to meeting Kurt Cobain, Courtney Love used to dance on its stage.

Love has actually been the perpetrator of a great many shenanigans in Vancouver, even after she met Cobain. While trying on clothes at a high-end Vancouver fashion store, she stormed out of the change room completely nude for seemingly no reason. She once unexpectedly jumped onstage during another's band set at the local club "Richards on Richards" (so named because the place is on Richards Street) to play a song, chewing off her fingernails first, so as to strum the strings better. Then, when she was finished, Love convinced the audience to let her play another song by lifting up her top and revealing her breasts.

But let's pretend Courtney Love isn't a famous person. Life just seems better that way. Bon Jovi's *Slippery When Wet* album was named for a sign that frontman Jon Bon Jovi saw while he was visiting the No. 5 Orange.

And Bon Jovi isn't the only celebrity to visit the strip club. Rock groups such as Aerosmith, Motlëy Crüe and AC/DC have partied at the club, as have athletes such as Charles Barkley, Dennis Rodman and Wayne Gretzky.

Lax Sex Laws

Vancouver has always had something of a laissez-faire attitude toward prostitution. The first red light district was at the shore of False Creek on a street creatively called Shore Street in the early 1900s, but the action was forced to moved during the construction of the Georgia Viaduct. Eventually, the women moved to the edge of Japantown, occupying a convenient spot between the city's poorest areas and the docks, where clientele was always at the ready.

For the most part, the police allowed the prostitution to happen, discouraging men from going to see the women rather than arresting the women for making themselves available. But there was little in the way of deterrence.

Once a handful of the city's conservatives and moralists began to put pressure on the police department, however, the officers responded with a brief crackdown. The largest prostitution bust in Vancouver history happened in 1912, when the police did a sweep of the city, arresting more than 200 johns and 100 madams. It didn't really change much; prostitution never left the area, and police returned to their laissez-faire practices shortly afterwards.

Unfortunately, the police were far too passive when it came to the prostitutes who were reported missing from the Downtown Eastside in the early 1990s and 2000s, and many were killed by pig farmer Robert Pickton, who preyed on the women for years. In December 2007, he was sentenced to life in prison for the second-degree murders of six women and charged in the death of 20 others. He allegedly told a cellmate that he had killed 49.

Police received multiple tips that Pickton had bodies in his freezer and that he had attempted to murder a woman in 1998, but they failed to intervene early, and as a result, far too many women died.

Hot Spots

There is one thing we don't need, and that is more fountains, because God has given us a perfectly wonderful supply of rain.

–Aeneas Bell-Irving, Vancouver alderman

INTRIGUING LOCATIONS

Sure, Vancouver is known for its skyscrapers, but some of its best places are a little closer to earth, at least in terms of height. But down to earth they ain't. You'd be hard-pressed, for example, to suggest that the Wigwam Inn was a sensible establishment. Sure, maybe it's owned by the Royal Yacht Club now, but back in the day, the inn was a haven for the rich and powerful, first owned by a suspected German spy. And then later things got more interesting.

Maybe these places don't tower like Vancouver's skyscrapers, but their tales might be taller.

Floored by These Floors

Located in Vancouver's West End, the high-rise apartment building is a second home to many of Vancouver's wealthy. It's also the source of one of the oddest sights in the city, as the roof of the 76-metre-tall building features a platform housing the head of a Douglas fir. It's a building with a tree growing out of it.

The tree sits atop the complex in homage to the Douglas firs that originally grew on the spot, before the Europeans arrived to cut the trees down and erect buildings such as this one in their stead.

Did I mention Eugenia Place is a home to the fabulously wealthy? Each 2700-square-foot apartment takes up an entire floor, one family apparently owns five, and many nights you can't see a light from the street because most of the building's tenants live someplace else.

All-in-one Store

The Old Hastings Mill Store Museum is the oldest building in BC, which might explain its storied history. These days, it's an out-of-the-way museum and heritage site, but in the late 1800s, it was a general store, a post office, a hospital and a morgue.

In 1865, Captain Edward Stamp secured the logging rights at the south shore of Burrard Inlet and established Hastings Mill on the site shortly afterwards. The store was the first building erected by the men who came to settle in the area. But don't think they threw it up hastily. It must have been incredibly well built because not only is the Hastings Mill store standing today, but it was also one of only five or six buildings in the early settlement that survived the Great Fire of 1886.

One reason for the building's good fortune was that it was literally on the water. While the mill sits on solid ground these days, it was initially built on stilts at the shore. After the fire subsided, the store was used to treat the injured and to house the bodies of those killed until they could be identified.

After the mill closed in 1929, there was some talk of tearing the old store down. However, the Native Sons of BC, one of Vancouver's early historical societies, recognized the value of the building and saved the old store by putting it on a barge and floating it to its present location. Their sister group, the Native Daughters, have been caring for the building ever since. The mill now functions as a museum.

The Native Sons of BC

The Native Sons of BC were a strange group—half historical preservation society and half racist cult. The group's members played a major role in salvaging the province's early history, successfully preserving not only the Old Hastings Mill Store but also the Nanaimo Bastion, now the premier landmark of

Nanaimo, Fort Langley, the site of BC's first settlement, and Craigflower School, the oldest schoolhouse in BC.

In the 1920s, the Native Sons successfully lobbied for the British Empire–oriented school system to teach local history and were instrumental in getting laws passed that protected totem poles, petroglyphs and other First Nations art.

However, while the group greatly respected the art of the First Nations community, they had much less kindness in their hearts for the people themselves. An incredibly racist group, the Native Sons of BC commissioned a series of paintings celebrating bloody triumphs over the Aboriginal population, vehemently opposed immigration and strongly backed the deportation of Asian citizens.

German Spies Make
Bad Business Partners

Accessible only by water, the Wigwam Inn, built in 1910, has little connection to the First Nations community after which it's styled. The brainchild of ad salesman Benny Dickens, who eventually attracted German businessman Alvo von Alvensleben as a business partner, the inn was built as a secluded, Native-themed, luxury resort for the rich and powerful.

Von Alvensleben certainly helped add some clout to the place. For much of the early 19th century, he drove British Columbian commerce. The German nobleman came to BC in 1904 and built one of the largest financial empires in the history of the province. He was a clever man, allowing many to suspect that he was a good friend of Kaiser Wilhelm's and that he was investing on both their behalf. The world's wealthy were intrigued by him, and any project with which he was involved was assumed to be a good one.

As a result, the Wigwam Inn attracted some impressive clientele. John D. Rockefeller and John Jacob Astor were among its visitors, staying at the Wigwam on April 15, 1911. One year later to the day, Astor drowned in the sinking of the *Titanic*.

But the Wigwam had a problem. Von Alvensleben's strategic willingness to let people assume he was connected to so many wealthy Germans eventually got the best of him. During a 1917 business trip to Poland, just as World War I was breaking out, von Alvensleben was arrested. British intelligence officials had sent a list of dangerous German spies to the U.S. Justice department, and his name had topped the list.

Although the allegations were never proven one way or the other, needless to say, the wealthy clientele stopped patronizing the Wigwam Inn, afraid to be aligned with a suspected spy. The inn began to lose money, eventually passed through the hands of a number of shady individuals and became a much less classy place to visit. In the 1950s, it was purchased by a man named Fats Robertson, and in the 1960s, he was charged with operating an illegal gambling club out of it.

The Wigwam Inn was well on its way to full-on dilapidation when the Royal Vancouver Yacht Club purchased it in 1986. It is now an exclusive outstation for club members.

Freaky Tiki

The Tiki Bar at the Waldorf, designed eight years after the hotel opened in 1955, boasts stools in the shape of old drums, tribal masks, fake palm trees, bamboo siding on the walls, illustrated island maps and a tropical mural near the restrooms. It's one of the oldest tiki rooms in the world; only San Francisco has one that predates it.

The artifacts that decorate the room aren't factory-made, either. Many are from the owner's trip to the South Pacific in the 1950s, including the painting of a nude Polynesian woman that hangs on one of the walls. But one element of the painting is inauthentic: the flower garland she wears, which hangs conveniently enough to censor her (although only slightly), was added after the painting found a permanent home at the Waldorf. Apparently, the BC liquor board took some offence to its explicitness, and when you run a bar, you need to keep those guys happy.

Explosive Stay

Built in the 1940s, the 2400 Motel is still in operation today despite almost looking older than it is. The motor court, which featured 19 white cottages and one of the coolest vintage signs in the city, has seen some incredibly interesting guests over the years, perhaps none moreso than Ahmed Ressam, a terrorist who stayed at the motel in December 1999, assembling ingredients for a bomb he intended to detonate at Los Angeles International Airport on the eve of the new millennium.

Unfortunately for Ressam, he was caught attempting to cross the U.S. border with more than 58 kilograms of explosive material, and his plan was thwarted.

Seedy Underground

In the summer of 2010, the 100-year-old building known as Maxine's was closed for good, brought down to make way for a new, 21-storey apartment building. It was a shame. Lost in the rubble was one of Vancouver's great crime hideaways. In its early days, Maxine's, named after Madam Maxine McGillvary, was a brothel, and a pretty darn good one at that. Gentlemen didn't just frequent Maxine's for the company—they went for a stiff drink as well.

The small house was long suspected to sit atop a network of secret tunnels that allowed rum- and drug-runners to sneak in their booze unsuspected, and the brothel drew some of North America's most notorious criminals. It was Vancouver's most successful house of debauchery.

It's said that two of America's most wanted baddies hid out at Maxine's for some time in the 1930s before J. Edgar Hoover learned their whereabouts and personally came to Vancouver to make the arrest. One got away.

While a number of establishments in the Vancouver area have long been suspected to be full of secret tunnels—most notably every building in Chinatown—Maxine's appears to have had two: one tunnel ran from English Bay to the house, and the other connected the brothel to Rogers Mansion, now the home of the renowned restaurant, Romano's Macaroni Grill. Both tunnels were boarded up a few years ago.

That's One Big Organ

The Orpheum was the biggest theatre in Canada when it opened in 1927, and it has been a staple of the Vancouver entertainment scene ever since. To this day, the theatre is one of the best places to hear live music. Although originally conceived as a vaudeville house, the end of vaudeville's heyday in the 1930s saw the Orpheum become primarily a movie house under Famous Players ownership for the next 40 years or so.

In the early 1970s, when Famous Players attempted to convert the theatre into a multiplex, the planned renovation sparked a public protest. Even Jack Benny flew in to support the "Save the Orpheum" movement, and in 1974, the theatre was saved when the city raised enough money to buy the building.

The Orpheum is full of unique flourishes. The catacombs beneath it are remnants of a massive, primitive, air conditioning system. The theatre is home to a $45,000 Wurlitzer 240 organ, which is the only original vaudeville organ in the world still operating in its original theatre. And finally, the plaster ceiling suspended by thousands of tiny wires houses a mural painted in 1976 by Tony Heinsbargen, one of the building's original painters. He painted most of the mural on canvas at his home in Los Angeles, then flew the artwork to Vancouver, where it was installed at the Orpheum as one would put up wallpaper.

OUTDOOR ADVENTURES

Stanley Park

When the city of Vancouver was officially formed in 1886, the first act of the city council was to set aside an 1000-acre military reserve for the establishment of Stanley Park.

The park has since become a major tourist attraction, as well as an icon of the coastal city. The beaches, the forest and stunning scenery are ideal for just about every outdoor activity you can name. But how did city council have the foresight to establish such a beautiful site? After all, they were looking at a vast stretch of wilderness, not a sprawling metropolis in desperate need of green space. Not to mention that most of the early settlers weren't overly concerned with preserving the natural beauty of the place —much of Stanley Park had already been logged in the 30 years before it was granted park status.

The city councillors were likely thinking of the present, not the future. If it seems unusual for a town of just over 2000 people to demand that so much land remain unsettled, that's because it was. But some ulterior motives may have been at play. By proclaiming the land untouchable, it forced settlers toward the massive land holdings the Canadian Pacific Railway had been given on the West End in exchange for selecting Vancouver as the CPR's western terminus. Thankfully, it worked out for everyone.

Stanley Park had far more land than the early Vancouverites even needed, which is one of the reasons the forest on the western side remains largely untouched. In the early days, the eastern side of the park saw plenty of development, with sports facilities installed, such as a cricket pitch, a lawn bowling green, a rugby field and a tennis court. But the park was so large that no one ever got around to bringing down the western forest, and by the time the city's population had grown enough to think about it, the forest was a staple of the park and further development was unthinkable.

False Creek, False Land

In 1916, looking for land on which to put a railway yard that would be competitive with the CPR, Vancouver's civic leaders hatched a plan: they would build the railway yard on the ocean. Of course, in order to do that, some draining had to be done. In Vancouver's early days, False Creek Inlet extended much farther inland. To get across Main, you had to cross a bridge from the Ivanhoe Hotel to 2nd Avenue, and everything beneath you was water and mud flats.

To make space for the railway yard, the city drained the creek. Over four years, 61 acres of marshland were drained and filled with dirt, and two railway stations were built on the land—the Canadian Northern and the Union Pacific. And then, after all that hard work was finally completed, the railway boom ended. Canadian Northern went out of business swiftly thereafter.

The next time you get off the West Coast Express at Pacific Central Station, consider that you're walking on what used to be the ocean. In fact, it still sort of is. During high tide, the basement has been known to flood.

Marpole Midden

While the settlement of Vancouver was established only in the late 19th century, it's believed the neighbourhood of Marpole, located on the southern edge of the city, directly across the Fraser River from the airport, was inhabited as long ago as 3500 BC. That's how far back researchers have dated some of the artifacts found in the Marpole Midden, one of the largest archaeological finds in North American history.

The trash receptacles of old civilizations, middens were pits dug in the ground to allow communities to dispose of their waste. But these sites also serve as archaeological safety deposit boxes, as the items buried in the earth yield all manner of clues about these early peoples. At 8.5 acres, the Marpole Midden remains the largest such treasure trove ever turned up in North America.

The site was found completely by accident, too. In 1889, as workers extended Granville Street to the southern edge, they unearthed the storehouse of treasures, finding weapons, tools, stone carvings as well as human remains, including what appeared to be evidence of a royal burial. In the 1930s, archaeologists mined the area thoroughly, turning up over 200 human skeletons. The area was declared a National Historic Site in 1933.

Deadman's Island

In 1862, early settler John Morton visited the small island to the south of Stanley Park with an eye toward purchasing it. He discovered hundreds of red cedar boxes hanging from the trees. What was in them? Morton soon found out when he stumbled across one that had fallen, spilling its contents: a jumble of human bones and black hair. Gross.

For whatever reason, Morton still wanted to purchase the island, but he was warned away by Chief Capilano, who explained to him that the island had been the scene of a battle in which nearly 200 men were killed and given a tree burial, and that it was therefore a dead man's ground. Morton decided against buying the island when he realized it might be teeming with malicious spirits. Always a wise decision. The island is named for Morton's story because, ironically, the Squamish merely called the place "Skwtsa7s," which means "island." How exciting. The Squamish languages are really bizarre when translated. Their words have punctuation and numbers in them. For example, "Squamish" is merely the English version of the band's actual name, which is "Skwxwú7mesh."

Because of the island's proximity to Stanley Park, there was some confusion over whether or not it was among the land protected when the park was set aside. This conflict hadn't been resolved by 1910, when moustache-twirling, logging magnate Theodore Ludgate leased the land in order to log it. Vancouverites were outraged, especially the people squatting on the island, and Mayor James Ford Garden wound up leading a citizens' march to prevent it from being cleared. The situation came to a head when Ludgate held an axe to a tree and Garden read him the riot act, threatening to arrest him if he were to "chop that tree." Ludgate did, and he was immediately arrested.

Unfortunately, Ludgate took the issue to court, won, and returned to log the island the following year. But then he went bankrupt. Serves him right.

Lost Lagoon: Neither Lost nor a Lagoon

Very few geographical locations in the Vancouver area are named by women, let alone women of First Nations descent, but Lost Lagoon is one of them. The lagoon, a body of water that sits on the edge of Stanley Park, was named in 1912 by poet Pauline Johnson.

Johnson, the author of *Flint & Feather*, one of the best-selling collections of poetry in Canadian history, used to write occasional articles for *The Daily Province*, now simply called *The Province*. She recounted Squamish legends, shared stories from the area's history, and, in one memorable piece, gave the lagoon its name. Up to that point, the lagoon had simply been part of Coal Harbour, a strange little inlet along the shore that confused the early explorers into thinking Stanley Park was an island. It was an honest mistake. At high tide, the waters of Coal Harbour crept well up the beach, creating a marsh that obscured a great deal of the surrounding land. At low tide, however, the marshland would vanish almost entirely. With this in mind, Johnson gave the marsh its name.

The name has actually never been accurate. Lagoons are full of saltwater and separated from the sea by a natural barrier that usually appears at low tide, but Lost Lagoon didn't receive that barrier until 1916, when the city created one. The plan had initially been to drain the lake and build a playground, but this would have cost $800,000. Instead, the city built the causeway for much less, turning the lagoon into a lake. Then, only six years later, in honour of Johnson, the city formally gave the lake the name Johnson had coined. Additionally, a monument was erected nearby in honour of her contributions to the city.

In the coming years, Lost Lagoon became less and less lagoon-like. In 1929, the city began plans to turn the area into a bird sanctuary. The pipes pumping saltwater into the lake were shut off, and the lake was filled with freshwater. Then, in 1936, the city drained the lake of its remaining saltwater to install a fountain, albeit not without controversy—the construction cost the city over $30,000. To avoid continued objection to the project during the Great Depression, installation of the fountain was exceedingly rushed, coming to completion in just a month.

I Like You, Have an Island

As mentioned earlier, there aren't a lot of places in Vancouver named after women (and substantially fewer when you rule out the Queen), but one area that stands out is Lulu Island, a large island located where the Fraser River runs into the Pacific Ocean. The island makes up most of the city of Richmond, a major suburb of Vancouver and the site of the Vancouver International Airport, although its eastern tip is actually part of New Westminster. Originally called "Island No. 1" in 1859, presumably because it was the biggest in the area, the site was given a new name by military colonel Richard Moody only a year later. He named it after a showgirl.

A fan of the arts, Moody and some of his fellow settlers had built a theatre in the early settlement of New Westminster. This attracted the San Francisco's Potter Theatre Troupe, the first such group to come into the area, and Moody was enchanted by 16-year-old Lulu Sweet, who sang and danced at the theatre. Moody accompanied Lulu and the troupe on the steamship to Victoria and flirted with her by pointing out the various landmarks along the way. When she asked about the name of the large island, Moody told her that it had no name, then paused, and immediately named it for her.

Moody was able to make the name stick because he had been appointed land commissioner in 1858. This wasn't the only time he abused his power for personal gain. Later that same year, Moody "sold" himself over 3750 acres in New Westminster. In July 1860, he was relieved of his responsibilities for the conflict of interest and shamed into selling much of this land to other settlers. He probably didn't mind. There's a nifty profit margin in selling things one stole.

DID YOU  KNOW?

Vancouver is home to a number of large Eastern populations, but here's one group you might not know about: squirrels. New York City has been the recipient of some famous gifts, most notably the Statue of Liberty from France, but it clearly hasn't learned much about the practice because the city is not the best giver itself. In 1909, they gifted Vancouver eight pairs of eastern grey squirrels, for reasons unknown.

A gift card might have been preferable. As it turns out, squirrels are the gift that keeps on giving. On any given day, you're sure to see one in Stanley Park, which is teeming with the little rodents. Grey squirrels are indigenous to the east, meaning each and every one you see in the park is a descendant of those original 16.

Ways to Get There

Vancouver is adopting a non-commercial approach.... I hope they have lots of money.

–Norman Thompson, English transit consultant

TRANSPORTATION STATION

Vancouver owes a great deal of its identity to transportation. In 1886, the city lucked out (or rather, made successful bribes), and the Canadian Pacific Railway decided to establish its major western terminus within its borders. Founded then and there on the future of transportation, Vancouver has been at the cusp of transportation ever since.

One hundred years later, the city celebrated its centennial at Expo '86 with a transportation theme, debuting the SkyTrain and placing it alongside Vancouver's other victories of transportation: the SeaBus and the Vancouver International Airport. The complete lack of a freeway in the downtown core only adds to the old-world charm of the city, but it also compounds the frustration of drivers.

But don't make the mistake of thinking that Vancouver has its transportation system all figured out. For a city with so many alternative transportation options, the traffic is still unbelievably congested. Worse, Aircare is a pain. And you'd think a progressive city like Vancouver would have gotten behind the Ballard fuel cell (especially since it might have done away with Aircare!), but you can't win 'em all.

SkyTrain

By the 1960s, it was apparent that Vancouver needed some sort of overhaul to the city's transit system. Traffic was at an all-time high, and a proposed freeway through the neighbourhood of Strathcona had just been voted down. A monorail system had been planned in the 1950s, but the project fell through before an architect could even be hired.

Finally, in 1980, Vancouver lucked out. The Urban Transportation Development Corporation had developed a new rapid transit technology, and the company was looking for a way to showcase the idea to the world. With the upcoming 1986 Expo in Vancouver, the municipality was glad to come together with the company on the project. The Expo line of the SkyTrain was completed just in time for the fair. The Millennium Line was completed in 2002, and the Canada Line opened in 2009.

The impact that the SkyTrain has had on Vancouver's downtown core is astronomical. Since the transportation system opened, the population living around it has increased by nearly 40 percent, and the population in its service area has more than tripled. More than $5 billion has been invested into the service area as well.

SeaBus

Perhaps the most pleasant trip you can take out of Waterfront Station is on the SeaBus to North Vancouver. The small ferry makes 126 10- to 12-minute trips a day, shuttling as many as 400 passengers across Burrard Inlet to North Vancouver's Lonsdale Quay.

The quay used to be the site of North Van Ship Repair, a major shipyard used during World War II to build and repair naval vessels such as the Bangor class minesweeper and the victory ship. Today, the quay is home to a public market and some of the city's best seafood.

The SeaBus carried its 100 millionth passenger in 2002, which is incredible when you consider that the project was nearly scrapped. The NDP government (which has a history of financial oversights when it comes to ferry projects in BC) began the project in the early 1970s and attracted controversy when the budget ballooned to over $35 million. The party lost power over the project, but by the time their successors took office, the SeaBus couldn't be halted without suffering a financial loss. Allowed to continue, the SeaBus has since become a beloved staple of Vancouver transportation, especially because of its reliability: the ferry has never missed a day of service.

Vancouver International Airport

Did you know that Vancouver's airport, which is considered to be one of the best in North America and has actually won an award to that effect twice in the past decade, was built out of embarrassment? In 1927, mayor L.D. Taylor tried to convince the famous aviator Charles Lindbergh to land the *Spirit of St. Louis* in Vancouver during his North American tour. Taylor was publicly embarrassed when Lindbergh refused on the grounds that Vancouver lacked a proper airport. "Your airport isn't fit to land on," the pilot sneered. This was true: at the time, all Vancouver had was a grass airstrip at the converted horse track in Minoru Park.

A year later, Taylor rode on the first flight from Victoria to Vancouver, landing on that very airstrip at Minoru Park. As he got out of the plane in front of a large crowd, he was struck by its propeller, suffering a fractured skull. A local pilot joked, "They say if he'd had an ounce more brains he'd have been a dead man."

While recuperating in the hospital, Taylor decided he was tired of being embarrassed by the city's pitiful airstrip. Shortly after he was released, he began looking for a plot of land on which to install a real airport, and only a year later, the city purchased space on Sea Island, not too far from Minoru Park.

William Templeton was named the airport's first manager before it was even built, and played a major role in its development. When told how much the American airport design firm was asking to be paid in exchange for drawing up the plans, he laughed, declined the quote and designed a plan himself for $14. Templeton's most lasting innovation was Cowley Crescent, the strangely curvy road that circles the first terminal. Why does it look that way? In a creative flourish, Templeton laid a light bulb down on the plans and traced it with a pencil.

DID YOU  KNOW?

On December 4, 1953, a Canadian Pacific Airlines commercial jet touched down at Vancouver International Airport at 12:42 AM. It wasn't the first plane to land at the airport, but it was notable because the flight had arrived non-stop from Tokyo. At the time, it was the longest commercial airline passenger flight in history. And no, they didn't show in-flight movies back then.

No One Wants a Cheap Car

With trains, skytrains, trolleys, boats, automobiles, buses and helicopters all passing through on a daily basis, it's easy to walk through Vancouver's waterfront station and recognize that the city has a long history of transportation. However, Vancouver has made contributions to the future of transportation as well.

Perhaps none is more intriguing than the Ballard Fuel Cell from Ballard Power Systems, a zero-emission proton-exchange-membrane cell that can power hydrogen-run cars and buses. The fuel cells combine hydrogen and oxygen to produce electricity and water. There is no pollution and the water is good enough to drink.

Unfortunately, the industry for this innovation never quite took off because hydrogen fuel was too expensive.

This wasn't the first time that Vancouver nearly revolutionized the automobile industry. In 1972, a Vancouverite named Blythe Rogers developed "The Rascal," the first energy-efficient car. The bright-orange, three-wheeled convertible was to sell for only $2700 and had almost 400,000 buyers lined up, but when financing fell through, production never started.

DID YOU KNOW?

In 1909, the city of Vancouver was proud to acquire the first mechanized ambulance in the province. They were so excited to be in possession of the vehicle that they took it out for a test drive. Unfortunately, the driver wasn't paying close attention to where he was driving and struck and killed an American tourist. It's too bad the tourist wasn't just wounded severely. Then they could have really put the ambulance to use.

The Flying Seven

In 1936, Edmontonian pilot Margaret Fane joined six other female pilots to form Canada's first ever all-female flying club. The idea was spawned after Fane went down to California and met members of the American all-female flying club, The 99s, including its president, Amelia Earhart.

Earhart suggested that Fane start a Canadian chapter of the club, and when Fane returned to Edmonton, she tried to do just that, but it soon became apparent that there simply weren't enough Canadian women flying planes to make the club feasible.

Eventually, Fane moved to Vancouver where she found six other young women with pilot licences: Rollie Moore, Betsy Flaherty, Tosca Trasolini, Jean Pike, Alma Gilbert and Elianne Roberge. The seven women united to form The Flying Seven in 1936.

The women hatched a plan to announce their arrival on the scene: the Dawn to Dusk Flying Patrol. For 11 hours, the women of The Flying Seven went out to prove "a woman's place is in the air," taking turns in the skies and always keeping a plane aloft. The stunt raised the profile of female aviation, leading many other women to discover the wonders of flight.

When World War II broke out in 1939, the experienced women pilots tried to join the Canadian Air Force but were refused. Still wanting to help the war effort, The Flying Seven took to the air locally, dropping leaflets all over British Columbia with a message encouraging donations, such as "Give Dimes or Dollars to Buy Our Boys More Planes." The women raised the huge sum of $100,000, which the Canadian Air Force used to purchase eight training planes.

The Sputnik Snafu

In 1961, newspapers around the world were hoping for a photo of *Sputnik*, the artificial satellite that launched the Space Age. Needless to say, *Vancouver Sun* publisher Don Cromie insisted that editor Hal Straight get one. With that, the photo department was sent into the sky in the largest plane available, a passenger jet, and instructed to get a photo of the Russian marvel.

They flew around the skies for some time, looking for anything they could see, but they couldn't spot *Sputnik*. Then photographer Dan Scott had a bright idea: maybe, he supposed, *Sputnik* was moving faster than the eye could see and would show up on the camera. With that hypothesis in mind, Scott pressed his camera to the window of the plane and shot a roll of film. Later, when he developed it back at the office, he was shocked to discover a brilliant flash of white in the dark of the night sky. He had indeed gotten the photo of *Sputnik*.

The *Sun* ran the photo on the front page as a world exclusive, eventually selling the shot to newspapers all over the globe. For quite some time, it was the definitive shot of the Russian satellite.

Later, however, Scott and the other *Sun* photographers realized that the dazzling flash of light was actually the flash from his camera reflecting against the window. Whoops.

It's tough to be too upset with Vancouver's newspapers when they get a little hasty. The competition in the city has always been fierce. In 1886, Vancouver had a population of about 1000, and yet, it also boasted three daily newspapers. Was there really that much news going on?

There were actually four papers if you count the *Moodyville Tickler*, which ran just across Burrard Inlet in the settlement of Moodyville. But it was hard to take the paper seriously, especially since it hardly took itself seriously. Launched in 1878, it was a strange little rag, often irreverent, and not overly concerned with journalistic integrity. The paper took donations, and the more you gave them, the better they made your obituary sound.

Aircare Blows

Few things infuriate Vancouver's automobile owners quite like the province's Aircare program, which requires all vehicles to undergo a diagnostic examination before they're insured.

No one disagrees with the idea of keeping high-emission vehicles off the road, but the practice can cause drivers to pull their hair out. If your automobile fails the test—which often feels completely random, what with beaters getting a pass while newer, seemingly problem-free vehicles fail, their owners handed an indecipherable grid as an explanation—it usually costs anywhere from $100 to $300 for the repairs.

If your vehicle insurance lapses while you're waiting for the appointment with your mechanic, you have to purchase temporary insurance that is far above the usual rates.

But that's not only an issue for irresponsible vehicle owners like myself. Aircare is just as meddlesome for serious owners of old and vintage cars, whose vehicles either have to be retired or adjusted to run differently than they were designed because they'll never pass otherwise. Many take their vehicles to mechanics for adjustments, pass Aircare and then readjust them immediately afterward.

Another way to get around Aircare is to register the vehicle out of province, in the Okanagan or on Vancouver Island, where Aircare is not required.

Standout Personalities

*One person in every 300 in
British Columbia is insane.*

—The Province

OUTSIDE-THE-BOX THINKERS

It simply isn't possible for a traveller to drift any farther west than Vancouver without sinking into the Pacific Ocean, meaning the city becomes the landing point of many wandering misfits. Throughout its history, from leadership on down, Vancouver has seen numerous oddballs, kooks and individualistic thinkers call its borders home. It's been said that British Columbia prefers its premiers "a little bit wingy," and that Vancouver boasts the highest rate of inventors per capita. People around here just think differently.

There's little in the way of a cohesive identity among the area's many citizens. That said, if Vancouver has a cohesive identity, it's in the consistent uniqueness of its residents.

Hard to Say, Really

Lululemon Athletica, a yogawear company founded by legendary Vancouver fashion retailer Chip Wilson, is one of Vancouver's largest-growing clothing brands. Wilson founded the company in 1998 in response to increased female participation in sports and in accordance with his belief that yoga was the optimal way to stay fit. The company offers free yoga classes, and Lululemon pants have become a staple of Vancouver fashion.

The story behind its name is an interesting one. While marketing his sportswear line, Homeless, to the Japanese, he discovered that a large part of the brand's appeal was the "L" in the name. Because the consonant doesn't factor in the Japanese language, it's difficult for them to pronounce, and the novelty added to the North Americanness of the product, giving it a unique appeal.

Upon realizing this, Wilson naturally jumped on the gimmick, weaving an "L" into as many of his women's sportswear line as he possibly could.

Reading Braille Road

The University of British Columbia features the largest Braille collection in the country, with over 6000 books in their library. All of these belonged to Charlie Crane, and he translated many of them. Crane attended UBC for two years, even starring on the varsity wrestling team, before going on to a career as a writer for *The Province*. All of this is remarkable when you consider that Crane was not only blind, but deaf. Seriously.

Charlie was born in Toronto in 1906 with all five of his senses, but he was stricken with spinal meningitis only nine months into his life, losing both his sight and hearing. At 10 years old, he was admitted to a school for the blind in Halifax, Nova Scotia, where he learned over 2000 words in six months. How? Charlie's first word was "come," taught to him by his teacher, Miss Conrod. He held one hand to her throat and the other to her lips and, through repeated trials, learned the two distinctive sounds in the word (the hard "C" and the hum of the "M") by touch. Charlie and Miss Conrod were able to increase his vocabulary meticulously from there, using the same tactic.

Lucky for Charlie, his sense of touch was remarkable. It's said that he once shook a preacher's hand and recognized the same man five years later when he shook his hand again.

Charlie and his family moved to Vancouver in 1921, and he immediately became the star pupil of Vancouver's School for the Blind, despite the obvious additional disadvantage. By the time he graduated from the small school, he was fully articulate and went straight into university.

He died in 1965, but not before planting the seeds of UBC's immense collection of tools for the visually impaired. Today, UBC's Crane Resource Centre and Library boasts an eight-studio book recording and duplicating facility, computers that convert print to synthesized speech and a computerized Braille transcription facility, among other resources.

Old Black Joe

Seraphim Fortes wound up in Vancouver after surviving a shipwreck in Burrard Inlet in September 1885. After thanking his lucky stars, the Barbados native settled in the city immediately. He made a home on English Bay, living in a tent and later a shack on the beach.

Fortes made his money through odd jobs such as shoe-shining and bartending, but his first love was lifeguarding. He spent nearly all of his free time on the beach, patrolling the waters and teaching children how to swim. He became a favourite among the kids of Vancouver, who called him either "Old Black Joe" or "English Bay Joe." Soon, the municipality recognized his work, naming Old Black Joe Vancouver's first official lifeguard.

Joe took the title seriously. He has been officially credited with saving 29 lives, though it's believed that he may have rescued over 100, and hundreds more if you count all the children he taught to swim. Many kids could do quality impressions of Joe's common refrain, "Kick yo' feet, Chile—kick yo' feet." But they never said it derisively.

Fortes remains one of the most beloved Vancouverites in the city's history. His funeral at the Holy Rosary Cathedra in 1922 remains the most attended in Vancouver to date, with thousands gathering outside to remember him. He was given a burial in Mountain View Cemetery, where his headstone simply reads, "Joe." Five years after his death, Vancouver's citizens dedicated a monument to him which bears the inscription "Little children loved him."

A branch of the Vancouver Public Library is named after him, as well as a popular restaurant opened on the 1985 centennial of his arrival to Canada. In 1986, he was named Vancouver's "Citizen of the Century."

Little Orpheum Ackery

In the summer of 1935, Ivan Ackery was named the manager of Vancouver's Orpheum Theatre, a position he held for the next 34 years. Taking over during the Great Depression, it took some serious innovation to convince people to come out to the theatre, but that wasn't a problem for Ackery. The man was one of the great managers in theatre history.

Under Ackery's management, the Orpheum was selected as the site of several national film premieres, most notably 1939's *Gone With the Wind*. Ackery also managed to draw some of the biggest acts of the day, with Louis Armstrong, Duke Ellington, Ella Fitzgerald and swingman Tommy Dorsey all performing at the Orpheum over the years.

But even when Ackery didn't have a great product, he had a great eye for marketing. He was a visible public figure, earning nicknames such as Mr. Orpheum, Atomic Ack and Little Orpheum Ackery, and he never passed up a cheesy stunt. He once paraded a cow down Granville Street wearing a sign that said, "There's a great show at the Orpheum and that's no bull."

Lily Laverock

Lily Laverock emigrated from Scotland to Vancouver with her family in the 1890s and played an active part in the city's activities. By the time Laverock retired in the early 1950s, she had played a pivotal role in the development of Vancouver's press, its music scene and equality for women. She was an original member of the University Women's Club that she helped found in 1907, as well as the Vancouver branch of the Canadian Women's Press Club that she established in 1909. A year after founding the Press Club, she became the first female reporter in Vancouver, taking a job with the *Vancouver World*. By 1918, she was the editor of the *News-Advertiser* at a time when very few females were reporters.

By 1921, she had established enough contacts and commanded enough respect that she began to work as an early concert promoter, of sorts. She brought in performers such as Geraldine Farrar, Sergei Rachmaninoff, and the Monte Carlo Ballet.

Laverock had a great sense of humour, too. When she retired, she sent a brief, 14-line biography to the papers, complete with a note that said, "It occurred to me that I might have some small obituary notice, and to have it correct, perhaps you could file this away for future use."

Red Robinson Rocks

Red Robinson is an icon in Canadian rock and roll, perhaps because he's the person who introduced the nation to this genre of music. Born in 1937 in Comox, Robinson found himself working in radio by the time he was 16 years old. Within two years, he was a staple of the local airwaves. What did he do that was so different? He played rock and roll music. He was the first Canadian disc jockey to do so.

Robinson became an ambassador for new music, introducing West Coasters to artists like Bill Halley and the Comets, Elvis

Presley and Buddy Holly. He even emceed concerts by Elvis and The Beatles when they played at Vancouver's Empire Stadium in 1957 and 1964, respectively. Robinson has worked at all sorts of radio and television stations, making an impact wherever he goes. *Trivia Challenge*, a television game show he hosted in 1971, served as the inspiration for the board game Trivial Pursuit.

In 1997, Robinson was elected to the Canadian Broadcast Hall of Fame, and in 2006, New Westminster's Red Robinson Show Theatre was opened in his honour. Although he "retired" from radio in 2001, he continues to broadcast his radio show in Vancouver.

Say "Cheese"...a Million Times

Over a 45-year photography career, Foncie Pulice took millions of photographs with his Electric-Photo camera. Many believe Pulice, a Vancouver native, took more photographs than anyone who ever lived.

A street photographer, Pulice simply walked up and down Granville Street taking photos of the passersby. In the early 1940s, servicemen and their families were tracking him down, desperate to get a family keepsake before they returned to war. Soon, Pulice was taking upwards of 5000 photos per day.

All across Canada, there are thousands upon thousands of Pulice's photos, some of people walking innocuously, others of people posing in the street. Pulice's camera is preserved at the Vancouver Museum, along with a slew of his photos.

POPULAR WEIRDOS

Painless Parker

Edwin R.R. Parker, known to many in the early 1900s as
"Painless Parker," was one of Vancouver's most famous dentists.
Far from a quiet practitioner, Painless Parker was something of
a dental showman. Inside his office on the second floor of
Vancouver's Sunrise Hotel, he would work in front of massive
windows that allowed spectators to witness his artistry. When
that didn't draw enough attention, he went out to the street and
set up a platform, inviting passersby to get free dental work.

Parker once claimed to have pulled over 350 teeth in one day, and he had a habit of wearing these teeth on a necklace. His motto was, "If it hurts, don't pay me," although one assumes that this motto was far from legally binding. Still, his unconventional practices must have worked, because Painless Parker owned several locations on Hastings and Granville streets.

I Find the Defendant…Sexy

North Vancouver's Gillian Guess has to be Vancouver's most famous (or infamous) juror. While sitting on the jury during the trial of accused murderer and druglord Peter Gill, Guess fell for the defendant, even trying to seduce him from across the court-room. According to court clerk Emma Hyde, "She would flip her hair and look seductive."

Gill's case is significant for two reasons. First, it's a really odd story. Second, it set legal precedents in three areas of Canadian law: it was the first case where a juror had sexual relations with a murder defendant after the trial (that we found out about… maybe it's a popular secret fetish?); it was the only case where a juror faced criminal sanction for the decision he or she made; and it was the only case in Canadian law where jury room discussions were made part of the public record.

Gill was acquitted in the initial trial, but when his relationship with Guess was uncovered, he was instead charged and jailed for obstruction of justice. Guess was charged with the same crime, leading to a trial that received international media attention, book and TV-movie deals, as well as an episode of *Law & Order*. It was the good *Law & Order*, too, back when Jerry Orbach was on it.

Guess seemed to enjoy the attention, launching a website full of ludicrous glamour shots and giving absurd sound bites such as when she claimed that she was being punished for falling in love. She also wore revealing clothing, big, fake Chanel sunglasses and bright lipstick. Guess was known to gasp during testimonies, insisted everyone call her "Gillian" instead of "the accused" and brought a dog to court.

Needless to say, the woman was a little strange.

Mr. Nobody

In November 1999, a young man checked himself into a Toronto hospital, the apparent victim of a mugging. He had no identification of any kind, the tags had been removed from his clothing, his nose was broken and he was unable to walk.

While the man wasn't sure of his name, he said that the name Philip Staufen floated to mind—perhaps that was it. He had a lush British accent, insisted on drinking tea from bone china and made a show of sitting for hours, reading sonnets. Suffice it to say, he became something of a media darling, dubbed "Mr. Nobody," and many people stepped up to help him. He was offered lodging with a British couple, which he accepted. He was also offered free treatment for his amnesia. This, he refused.

What he really wanted was a Canadian passport, and in November of the following year, he came to Vancouver lobbying to be granted Canadian citizenship and a Canadian birth certificate so that he could travel in search of his true identity. He procured the services of a lawyer named Manuel Azevedo, who lobbied on his behalf. In May 2011, a BC court denied his petition, but on June 5, Minister Elinor Caplan offered him a Mister's Permit to stay and work in Canada for 18 months. He refused this too. He instead announced a hunger strike until his needs were met.

His story began to unravel that summer. On June 15, a man named Sean Spence, the editor of a gay magazine, claimed that Staufen was actually a French porn model named Georges Lecuit, and that the two had worked together in Britain. Spence provided convincing photographic evidence, though Staufen denied the claims. Still, Staufen had been suspiciously good-looking, well manicured and tanned for quite some time. If he wasn't already a former gay porn model, it was a future worth looking into.

Among the many who found Staufen beguiling was Nathalie Herve, the daughter of his lawyer. The two married in mid-July, at which point Nathalie's father resigned as Staufen's lawyer. The couple moved to Ottawa, then Montréal, then Halifax.

In 2004, it emerged that George Lecuit had reported his passport stolen in 1998. It became apparent how Staufen had gotten to Canada, and he was arrested and jailed. Upon his release, Staufen and his wife disappeared.

So who was he really? The *National Post* found a former friend of Staufen's who said the man he had known in London as Georges Lecuit had once admitted to being from a poor Romanian family. CBC's *The Fifth Estate* had managed to track down a Romanian woman who claimed that Staufen was her son, with a birth certificate to prove it. Finally, confronted with the certificate, Staufen admitted to GQ magazine that he was born Ciprian Skeid in Timisoara, Romania, and that the story had been a hoax.

Dancing Machine

It just makes sense that an eclectic city like Vancouver would be home to one of the last licensed jesters in the Western world. In 1968, the Canada Council for the Arts awarded a $3500 grant to entertainer Joachim Foikis, who sought to revive "the ancient and time-honoured tradition of the town fool."

Foikis was a popular character in Vancouver in the late 1960s. He attended city council meetings in a full jester's costume (including a cap and bells), often rising to recite nursery rhymes. He danced up and down the sidewalk, interacting with anybody and drawing laughs from the crowd. He was a mainstay at outdoor events and was welcomed when he turned up unexpectedly.

But it wasn't all fun and games. Foikis was notoriously outspoken, rallying against the bureaucracy that supported the wasteful Vietnam War and warning passersby of impending nuclear destruction.

His death, while shocking and sad, was an appropriate one for a jester. In 1972, while dancing on a precipice above a stage at Victoria harbour where a band was playing, he lost his balance and fell from the great height. In other words, he died dancing.

Nardwuar, the Human Serviette

Few Vancouver personalities are more memorable than Nardwuar, the Human Serviette, an interviewer who wears a plaid golfing outfit. Nardwuar's interviewing style is beyond eclectic, as he speaks in an incredibly high-pitched voice, spouts non-sequiturs, asks incredibly bizarre, rapid-fire questions and gives obscure records to his subjects.

Nardwuar has other quirks as well. He's something of a guerrilla interviewer, often descending on his subjects unannounced. But he also does extensive research and can bring up minutiae about artists' pasts, and he ends every interview with "Keep on rockin' in the free world," then says, "doot doola doot doo." He is usually unwilling to let his subjects go until they finish the refrain with "doot doo."

It's safe to say that Nardwuar is not to everyone's tastes. While some love him, such as rappers Pharrell Williams and Jay-Z, Nardwuar has gotten under the skin of some pretty big names. Musicians Beck and Alice Cooper have told him off, Kid Cudi and Slipknot walked out on their interviews and Quiet Riot chased him down the street.

In one of his more memorable interviews, in November 1997, Nardwuar cut off all his hair and was able to sneak into an APEC conference to ask Jean Chrétien if he supported the pepper spraying of protesters outside. Chrétien's response, "For me, pepper, I put it on my plate," is a famous line in Canadian political history.

UNIQUE GROUPS

The Vancouver Lego Club

The Vancouver Lego Club (VLC), an organization for discerning Lego enthusiasts, meets once a month to showcase the handiwork of its members and exchange ideas, inspirations, bricks and sets. The VLC is one of around 40 adult Lego leagues in the world.

The club's goals are to provide an atmosphere conducive to the admiration, appreciation and sharing of Lego, to form an organization of energetic and creative individuals who wish to exchange ideas and information concerning Lego, to publicly extol the virtues of Lego via public displays of LEGO creations and to represent The Lego Company and its products in a productive, enjoyable and educational light in the hopes of inspiring new Lego enthusiasts.

One imagines that having fun playing with children's toys is also a goal.

Vancouver Magic Circle

There are few better places to practice magic than Vancouver, home to the Vancouver Magic Circle (VMC), one of the world's largest rings for professional and amateur magicians. Members of the VMC meet once a month at the Sunrise Community Hall to talk shop, encourage one another and share tricks of the trade.

The club was formed in 1942, after established magicians and good friends Charles Howard and William Shelly brought together about a dozen other magic enthusiasts from the area. Howard, a retired army captain, served as the club's first president and begun amassing literature for the Vancouver Magic Circle Library. The collection has grown to become one of the largest Magic Libraries in North America—it contains over 2000 volumes and increases daily. In 2010, 400 books were added to the library's shelves.

Shelly served as the VMC's second president and established the club's first newsletter. The *Magical Minutes* released its inaugural issue in 1944 and continues to publish issues to this day.

The Silk Riot

One of Vancouver's strangest riots was because of silk. By 1940, Saba's, a silk company started by Lebanese merchants Michael and Alexander Saba, was the largest retail house in Western Canada specializing in silks. The store was exceedingly popular among the city's women during a time when stockings were a must-have.

But World War II made it difficult for Saba's to import the fabric, and demand for silk stockings reached absurd levels. When a shipment of 300 nylon stockings arrived in 1942, over 500 women rushed to the store to get a pair. The result was a scene that turned violent in a hurry. Thankfully, no one was hurt, but a lot of women went home without new stockings, which may have been worse.

Adbusters

The Occupy Wall Street movement took the world by storm and saw thousands of protesters in Vancouver do just that on September 17, 2011, marching into Zuccotti Park and taking up residence. The protesters' slogan, "We are the 99%," referred to the growing difference in wealth in the United States between the wealthiest one percent and the rest of the population.

The movement was the brainchild of the Adbusters Media Foundation, a not-for-profit, anti-consumerist organization founded and based in Vancouver. They are responsible for and perfectly described by the term "culture jamming," which is the act of subverting or disrupting mainstream cultural institutions. That's what Adbusters does. The group has been publishing a reader-supported, advertising-free magazine called *Adbusters* since 1989, and they have launched numerous international campaigns.

While Occupy Wall Street has garnered the most attention, Adbusters is also responsible for Buy Nothing Day, an international day of protest against consumerism that happens to share a date with Black Friday, and TV Turnoff Week, which is exactly what

it sounds like and takes place over the crucial ratings period known as "sweeps."

In addition to these activities, Adbusters has purchased anti-consumerist billboards in Times Square, placed full-page ads in the *New York Times* and filmed high-concept, anti-consumption commercials in order to spread their message. The magazine has some big fans—Tim Robbins, Sean Penn and Bruce Springsteen are subscribers.

Greenpeace

These days, Greenpeace is a massive, international environmental organization that brings in nearly $200 million a year, but at one time, it was just a small Vancouver environmental group. Greenpeace was founded in a storefront in Kitsilano to oppose the U.S. testing of nuclear devices in Amchitka, Alaska, which many believed would cause earthquakes and potentially a tsunami.

When America tested the device and no earthquakes or tsunamis occurred, the country announced that it was going to detonate five more powerful bombs, and a small group of protesters grew tired of the lack of action. The group hatched a plan to sail a boat up the coast and publicly oppose the military tests.

Supported by folk singer Joan Baez, a benefit concert took place at the Pacific Coliseum in Vancouver on October 16, 1970, and the group raised enough money to charter a ship, the *Phyllis Cormack*, and set sail for Amchitka. For the voyage, they renamed the ship *Greenpeace*, a term coined by activist Bill Darnell, and the organization took on the same name.

After the U.S. was finished its testing, *Greenpeace* turned its eye to the French Navy's weapons testing at the Moruroa Atoll in French Polynesia. It was there that the group connected with a young, Vancouver-born businessman named David McTaggart, a wealthy man who owned his own yacht and was willing to sail it in protest of France's practices. During these protests, McTaggart was allegedly beaten badly enough to lose sight in one eye, and when the assault went public, France backed off the testing.

Trailblazers

What is the meaning of this aggregation of filth?

> –Captain James Raymur, upon
> moving to Gastown in 1869

FUNNY FOUNDERS

You don't settle in Vancouver unless you're a little odd, and that's certainly a safe observation. Many of Vancouver's greatest trailblazers were also exceedingly strange men, with bizarre quirks that might not have flown any place else— unusual hangups that went unnoticed among other oddballs and immense character flaws that were forgiven in settlements simply looking for people, any people.

How many places, for example, would anoint a man who changed his name to Amor de Cosmos to be their premier and who also had a penchant for public outbursts of emotion?

Or what of Matthew Begbie, who never met an American he wouldn't hang, and once cussed out his own jury for denying him the opportunity? I can assure you that in no other city but Vancouver could such a man be given power of execution. And let's not forget Gassy Jack, who was allowed to open an illegal saloon with free labour from local miners on land he didn't own.

Because of where they came from and the era in which they arrived, these men were considered founders. In most other places in time, they'd be patients. They lucked out.

The Three Greenhorns

It's incredible to think that the three men who purchased the first lots in Vancouver's West End, now the most densely populated portion of the Lower Mainland (and among the wealthiest), were roundly mocked for the purchase. In June 1862, Samuel Brighouse, William Hailstone and John Morton arrived in New Westminster looking for a place to mine coal. After seeing a piece of coal in a shop window, they asked for a tour of the inlet and found themselves drawn to the West End. Soon, the three made purchases of 180 acres each—the maximum allowable amount—for just over $550.

They were laughed at for the purchase, which was deemed far too much for such worthless land, and many in the surrounding area took to calling them "The Three Greenhorns." A rumour spread that the coal had been placed in the shop window as a ruse designed to trick some sucker (or suckers) into buying the very land the men now owned.

The greenhorns never saw much success on the West End. They went into brickmaking, only to discover demand for brick was scarce at the time. They tried to sell others on moving into the area and developing a community, but nobody was interested. Eventually, they were convinced to donate a third of their land to the Canadian Pacific Railway in exchange for the CPR establishing its western terminus in the area and making it a major stop, but they were frustrated when the dividends weren't immediate.
All three left the area. Hailstone sold his share to Brighouse for $20 and returned to England; Brighouse purchased a farm in Burnaby; and Morton went to California in search of gold.

Although they'd never quite realize it, were it not for their donation and foresight, the city of Vancouver wouldn't be what it is today. In 1967, a sundial was erected at English Bay in honour of the Three Greenhorns.

Amor de Cosmos

Born in Nova Scotia on August 20, 1825, William Smith headed west during the California Gold Rush and wound up settling in British Columbia. He was a famously eccentric man who had unusual phobias, such as a fear of electricity, bursting into tears in public and a wild temper that led to several fistfights. He never married, had few friends and was known for his tendency to flout conventions. Seemingly unhappy with his name during his days in California, Smith successfully petitioned the California State Assembly to change his name to "Amor de Cosmos," translated roughly as "lover of the universe." Maybe that's why he never married—he was already romantically involved with the universe.

De Cosmos had numerous jobs: first as a gold prospector, later as the editor of the *Daily British Colonist*—now known as the *Victoria Times-Colonist*—and in 1872, as the second premier of British Columbia.

De Cosmos, who had a heightened sense of nationalism, played a major role in the development of British Columbia. His belief that the colonies of British North America needed to be self-supporting, develop a distinct identity and form a political and economic union led to the two great causes of his later career: the union of Vancouver Island and British Columbia, which happened in 1866, and the Colony of British Columbia's entry into Confederation. To advance these causes, de Cosmos left journalism and entered politics.

While de Cosmos claimed to love the entire universe, he was actually pretty racist, and it's the major reason he didn't become

the first premier of British Columbia. He despised the idea that
"they make themselves hated wherever they go."

Needless to say, the black population of Vancouver Island, which
was quite large, took offense to his statements, especially just
before the election. They voted against him in a block and he was
defeated in 1874, which likely drove him nuts.

Two years before his death in 1897, his eccentricities intensified,
and he was declared insane.

It is rumoured that, while in California, Amor de Cosmos was the first person to suggest using photography to take pictures of naked people. Considering how popular the practice is in California these days, that would make Amor de Cosmos the father of porn. No wonder he wanted to be known as the lover of the universe.

The Hanging Judge

Born in 1819 on the isle of Mauritius, Matthew Begbie came to British Columbia in the 1850s and served as the first chief justice of the BC Supreme Court from 1870 until his death in 1874. People called him "British Columbia's first citizen" because he was the first man to enforce a certain ethic of citizenship. He travelled throughout the province on foot and later horseback, administering justice in incredibly informal settings, although he is said to have always worn his judicial robes and wig when court was in session.

Begbie took the law incredibly seriously. Determined to prevent the same sort of lawlessness that had pervaded the California Gold Rush, Begbie enforced the law strictly in the north. The death penalty was mandatory in murder cases in those days, unless the government approved a judge's recommendation for clemency, which meant a great deal of hangings occurred. Americans were especially targeted because they came north expecting the same licence to kill that they enjoyed down south. Begbie came to be known as "The Hanging Judge."

Begbie wasn't simply a bloodthirsty avenger, however. He was a man of his convictions. He successfully lobbied for a number of men who he felt were falsely accused to be granted leniency, and he also once famously voiced his disgust when a jury in Cariboo went easy on a man he clearly believed to be guilty of far worse.

"Had the jury performed their duty," he told the released man, "I might now have the painful satisfaction of condemning you to death, and you, gentlemen of the jury, you are a pack of Dallas horse thieves, and permit me to say, it would give me great pleasure to see you hanged, each and every one of you, for declaring a murder guilty only of manslaughter." Okay, maybe he was a tad bloodthirsty.

Begbie was also the presiding judge over the first case of a white man assaulting a Native man. Granted, there had been many other instances of this type of assault, but Begbie was the only one who felt a need to make a federal case out of it—or maybe it was because he was the lone man who could. Begbie was able to speak several languages. He could understand the First Nations man's testimony without the use of an interpreter. The judge also authorized the man to swear on an item he held sacred in place of the Bible. The white man was found guilty.

An American once criticized Begbie's penchant for hanging, and Begbie obliged him, appropriately, with some gallows humour. "I never hanged any man," Begbie said. "I simply swore in American citizens like yourself, and it was you who hanged your fellow countrymen."

DID YOU KNOW?

John Robson is the man after whom Vancouver's renowned Robson Street is named. He became the ninth premier of British Columbia in 1889, and he died in office. How did he die? While visiting London in June 1892, he shut the door of a carriage on his finger and later died of blood poisoning in the hospital.

Junk Collector

Vancouver's first hoarder was Major James Skitt Matthews, who settled in the city in 1898. He immediately showed a passion for collecting and cataloguing artifacts and stories of the city's history. The archives began in his home, but the City soon gave him space in a number of locations, one of which was the attic of the old City Hall building in the early 1930s.

The room was said to be the dirtiest in all of British Columbia, a dark, dank place without heat, water or light, and cluttered with all sorts of historical material. But clearly, Matthews' willingness to spend so much time on the archives impressed the mayor, because after two years working in the attic, Matthews was named the city's official archivist. He was even paid a salary of $25 a month.

Shortly thereafter, when new mayor Gerry McGreer completed construction on the new City Hall and made plans for the migration, the two men had a dispute over the archived material's worth (McGreer felt Matthews was just a junk collector) and who it belonged to, and Matthews wound up moving the collection back into his home.

Matthews collected so much material over his lifetime that, when he died in 1970, the City of Vancouver built a building especially to house it all. When the Major Matthews Building opened in 1972, it was the first building in Canada built specifically as a city archive. The semi-underground structure in Vanier Park now serves as the repository for historical records generated by nearly every public office in the city, and contains numerous collections from private donors, businesses and community groups. These days, the artifacts are kept very clean.

Gassy Jack

John Deighton, the resourceful bar owner who opened the city's first tavern, the Globe Saloon, was known to the locals as "Gassy Jack" because he had a penchant for storytelling.

But don't think the man was just a big blowhard. He was also a clever opportunist, joining the Cariboo Gold Rush, only to discover that he wasn't all that good at finding gold. He quickly abandoned the career and instead moved into bartending, opening the first saloon in New Westminster in 1862. He made a pretty penny until July 1867, when he left the saloon in the care of an American friend while he went to visit a doctor down the river.

Unfortunately for Deighton, he was gone over the Fourth of July, and his friend, being the patriot that he was, spent all of Gassy Jack's cash on gunpowder, rockets and fireworks, and gave away all the liquor for free during the celebration. When Jack returned, he was broke. One assumes he stopped hanging out with the American fellow.

Worse, the gold was drying up and the prospects were moving on, meaning the bar owner had little chance of making his money back. He had to find a new place to set up shop. Seeing the success of Hastings Mill to the west, and at the behest of his friend, Captain Edward Stamp, who owned the mill, Jack took his canoe up Fraser River.

He had little when he arrived, save a few pieces of furniture, a yellow dog, $6 and his Native wife, but Gassy Jack was able to get his saloon built by promising the off-duty mill workers all the whisky they could drink in one sitting once he opened. With the nearest drinking hole 40 kilometres away at the time, the promise of a local watering hole and a night's worth of free booze was too good for the workers to pass up. The Globe Saloon was constructed in an astonishing 24 hours. A community soon built up around it, and the bar became the nucleus of early Vancouver. Until the city was given its official name, the settlement was unofficially called Gastown for several years.

At some point, someone realized that Jack didn't own the land on which his makeshift establishment rested, and he had to move down the street. But he had a little more money to his name than when he had arrived so bought the nearest plot of land and built an impressive new saloon, a two-storey building he named the Deighton Hotel. The building stood for only 12 years, unfortunately; it was lost in the Great Fire of 1886.

Jack passed away in 1875. His last words were: "Damn that dog. I wish he'd shut up."

DID YOU  KNOW?

If you're on the hunt for BC collectibles, the rarest of the rare is a set of 1862 British Columbia $10 and $20 gold and silver coins. Minted during the Fraser Gold Rush as a way to convert the gold to currency, these coins were never actually issued after Governor James Douglas decided they simply weren't necessary. And yet, somehow, the coins found their way into the hands of government ministers such as former premier John Robson, for whom Vancouver's iconic Robson street is named. How? They were given as gifts. But nowadays nobody's giving these coins out for free. They could fetch $200,000 or more at auction.

Letters in Prison

Not only was the famously relaxed Jonathan Miller Vancouver's first postmaster, but before that, he was the tiny community's only peace officer. He lived in the lone public building in the village, a small cottage next door to Gassy Jack's Globe Saloon, and ran a two-room prison out back. When Granville became Vancouver in April 1886, this same building served for a while as the first city hall.

Miller was assisted for several years by a man named John Clough who acted as the jailer and was also the city's first and only lamp-lighter. Downtown Vancouver's Lamplighter Pub—the first British Columbia establishment to obtain a liquor licence and the first to serve to women—is named with Clough in mind. If you think about it, it's amazing that Clough had two jobs, especially one that required a great deal of strong-arming and another that involved a steady hand, given that he had only one arm.

If you found yourself spending the night in Miller's prison, usually because of drunken or lewd behaviour after a night at the saloon, you weren't going to get much rest and he cared very little about your hangover. His prisoners were sent out each morning on a chain gang to clear land and maintain roads, watched over by Clough and occasionally even an armed guard. Miller's skill at keeping the peace made him an ideal candidate to be Vancouver's first police chief, but by then, he was much too enamoured with being the postmaster. The peace he preferred to keep was his own. He held the position until his retirement in 1909 at the age of 75.

The Mayor Was a Crook

L.D. Taylor was the city's 14th, 17th, 22nd and 24th mayor. He lost many mayoral elections, but he also won seven between 1910 and 1934. In 24 years as a mayoral candidate, Taylor served as mayor for 11.

Taylor rose to prominence in Vancouver as a newspaperman, buying the *Vancouver World* and commissioning the Sun Tower —then called the "World Building"—to house it. When it was completed in 1912, it was the tallest building in the British Empire, and remains a Vancouver landmark to this day. Taylor also oversaw the development of Vancouver's first airport and was instrumental in amalgamating South Vancouver, Vancouver and Point Grey. In short, without L.D. Taylor, Vancouver would look quite different.

It's ironic that Taylor was a newspaperman because many of his scandals filled the pages of *Vancouver World*. He went through a handful of messy divorces and was briefly married to two different women at the same time. He allegedly had connections to a number of the city's brothel owners and bootleggers, and he did little to dispel these allegations, claiming that the city should focus on the prevention of major crimes, not vice crimes, and that he had no intention of running a "Sunday school town." In this sense, he may have contributed to Vancouver's laissez-faire attitude regarding marijuana, among other things.

It's unsurprising that Taylor was comfortable with the city's shady elements: he actually had a secret shady past. Born in Michigan,

Taylor worked as a Chicago accountant until 1896, when he was 39. Why would he immigrate to Canada so late in his life? Unbeknownst to anybody, he was about to be indicted on charges of bank fraud. Despite being a public figure, he somehow managed to keep this a secret during his entire life in Canada.

DID YOU  KNOW?

Vancouver isn't just green; it's got a shady history. Its status as the largest city in British Columbia is the direct result of a backhanded business deal cut between British Columbia Premier William Smithe and the Canadian Pacific Railway. In 1885, the CPR was looking for a Western terminus, and many felt that the company would select either the settlement in Port Moody, which lay at the head of Burrard Inlet, or the one in New Westminster, which was already a fairly established city. Instead, the CPR threw a curveball, unexpectedly selecting Vancouver.

Why? Because Smithe made the CPR an offer they couldn't refuse, promising the railway 6000 acres of free land on the city's west side if they chose to set up shop there instead.

Think He Had Blisters?

In July 1862, a man named Maximilian Michaud arrived in Burrard Inlet. The 30-year-old had come all the way from Montréal *by foot*. You'd think that after walking the entire way, he might have been tired, but Michaud showed no signs of fatigue. Shortly after arriving, he marched right into the New Brighton Hotel and purchased it from its owner, Mr. Oliver Hocking.

Michaud renamed the business the Hastings Hotel and turned it into a popular hotspot. For a time, it was the best place in the settlement to drink, and though it was illegal to sell liquor to the

First Nations people in the area, Michaud exercised no discretion to whom he served.

But the building was popular for another reason as well: it was the settlement's first post office. Considering Michaud's penchant for walking, it's no surprise he took over postmaster duties not long after strolling into town.

Vancouver Showbiz

*I've never seen so much coffee in all my life.
The whole town is on a caffeine jag, and still
nothing gets done any faster.*

–Bette Midler, during a Vancouver
concert performance

FAMOUS VISITS

With all the ways to get into town and all the money in it, Vancouver has been blessed with the opportunity to play host to several the world's greatest stars: Sarah Bernhardt, Elvis and The Beatles, among others.

It doesn't always go so well. Sure, success stories occur, where the star comes to town, is treated like a star and falls in love with the community. That happens fairly regularly. But it's just as common to see residents get a little too excited and froth at the mouth, chasing the star right back to the airport. Other times, Vancouverites don't quite realize what they're seeing and shun a legend, as they once did with Bernhardt.

Sometimes, Vancouver isn't at fault for a celebrity visit gone wrong. It's possible that the star got too wrapped up in all the sights and sounds of downtown and spent the visit on a bender, or worse, in a hospital. All of these incidents have happened and will happen again.

Vancouver, City of Chivalry

Vancouver was a great deal more receptive to Russian dancer Anna Pavlova, the first ballerina to tour the world and among the most famous dancers who have ever lived. She came to Vancouver on November 17, 1910, and danced before a full house. Reviews were positively sublime. The city went mad for her, perhaps because she didn't speak French.

After her performance, Pavlova went out for dinner, only to discover the restaurant she had chosen was packed. She was immediately offered several tables by smitten fans, and when she took one, a man stood up and made a rousing speech in her honour before asking everyone to drink to her health. According to Pavlova, the scene made the papers and word travelled down south. When Pavlova followed soon afterwards, men on her tour stops tried to outdo the courtesy Vancouver had shown. She was smothered in chivalry and applause at every turn.

Though Pavlova passed away in 1931, her final interaction with the city that adored her came in 1940, when the Empress Theatre, where she had performed during one of her three stops in town, was torn down. As the workers picked through the debris, one of them noticed a tiny powderpuff and bent down to pick it up. The word "Pavlova" was stitched on it in faded gold letters.

The Lost and Found in the CBC Archives

If I had the time, I'd spend a couple months down in the basement of the CBC building, combing through the archives of the broadcast company. Deep beneath the building, hidden away in a couple of rooms, are all sorts of remarkable pop culture treasures: silent movies, recordings of old radio dramas and footage of some amazing local concerts.

Two such concerts have been lost, however: in August 1964, The Beatles played one of only a handful of shows in Canada, performing at Vancouver's Empire Stadium to a crowd of over 20,000 screaming fans. It was apparently difficult to hear much over the shrieks of the audience, but although there wasn't much to hear, there was plenty to see: the crowd inside the stadium was unruly, leading emcee Red Robinson to interrupt the show and plead with the audience to calm down.

Robinson's pleas didn't work, as thousands of teenagers rushed the stage, crushing hundreds of young girls against the restraining fence and leaving dozens with broken ribs. To make matters worse, for his troubles, John Lennon told Robison to "Get the f*** off the stage."

Even outside the stadium, the situation had gotten out of hand, as fans made three attempts to smash the 10-foot high stadium gates. The third time was the charm, and a number of fans got into the stadium before police and ushers pressed against the gate to hold it shut.

The Beatles found the crowd unsettling, only playing for 27 minutes before leaving the stadium. Worse, the footage of the Fab Five's only visit to Vancouver was lost almost instantly: someone erased over the tapes the next day.

The other concert footage that has mysteriously disappeared was Elvis Presley's show on August 31, 1957. It was only the second rock and roll show in Vancouver's history, after Bill Haley and the Comets, and far and away the largest at the time, drawing over 24,000 people. Unsurprisingly, Elvis's visit yielded pretty much the same scene as The Beatles did. The King played for only 22 minutes before getting spooked by the crowd and making a quick escape from the venue.

Although it's unfortunate that concert footage of Elvis and The Beatles at Empire Stadium has been lost, the CBC archives still harbour over 155,000 film clips. I'm sure there's plenty more worth watching.

DID YOU KNOW?

U.S. president Bill Clinton visited Vancouver for the 1997 APEC conference, purchasing a marble bear's head from Hill's Indian Crafts. The sculpture turned up later in court documents as a gift he gave to his mistress Monica Lewinsky.

Parlez-Vouz Anglais?

Sarah Bernhardt has often been referred to as the most famous actress the world has ever known. She was a pioneer of silent movies, starring in eight of the first French films, but before that, she was a star of the stage, in high demand everywhere she went.

Vancouverites had heard great things about Bernhardt, and they were beyond excited when she made a weeklong appearance in Vancouver, giving six performances of *Camille* and six of *Du Théâtre du champ d'honneur*. Tickets, which ranged from 15 to 80 cents a head, sold out on the first night. After that, however, attendance dropped off steeply. How come? Did she have an off night? Was she dreadfully overrated? No. She was just French.

For whatever reason, Vancouverites assumed her performances would be in English. When word spread that they were not, people stopped going to her show.

How the Grinch Built the PNE

In 1910, a young man named William Pratt arrived in Vancouver. He had come to Canada in search of an acting career, but in the meantime, he needed to eat, so he took odd jobs wherever he could

get them. This led him all the way across the country, with stops in Toronto, Montréal, Banff and then Vancouver, where he laid streetcar tracks, shovelled coal and worked as a land surveyor. Then he found steady work as a carpenter, helping to build the grounds for Vancouver's first Pacific National Exhibition in 1910.

Pratt made enough money to make a trip to Hollywood. He changed his name to Boris Karloff and became one of the great actors in horror film history, best known to many for his iconic role as Frankenstein's monster. Others still likely remember him as the narrator of the animated television special, 1966's *How the Grinch Stole Christmas*.

Partied Out

Australian-born actor Errol Flynn, the star of such films as *The Charge of the Light Brigade* and *The Adventures of Robin Hood*, among others, visited Vancouver in October 1959. The 50-year-old was only in town to lease his yacht to millionaire friend George

Caldough, but he decided to kick back and stay awhile. Unfortunately, he kicked back too hard and never left.

Flynn's party started early—apparently, he threw up on the plane from Los Angeles—and lasted for six days. He and his 17-year-old girlfriend stayed at the Hotel Georgia but spent most of their time at local nightclubs like the Cave, the Panorama Roof and the Penthouse. On the sixth day, the couple headed to the airport to return home when Flynn suddenly began to complain about back pain.

They wound up in the West End apartment of Dr. Grant Gould, brother of pianist Glenn Gould. Somehow, another party started, and at some point during the evening, Flynn went to the bedroom for a nap, announcing to the guests, "I shall return." He did not. A few hours later, his girlfriend found him dead.

According to local lore, the partygoers propped him up in the lobby, so as to continue the party. This is a myth. It's hard to believe if you read the coroner's report, too: according to the death certificate, Flynn died of liver sclerosis, liver degeneration, coronary thrombosis, diverticulitis of the colon and myocardial infarction, among other maladies. In short, he was all partied out.

Stick to the Jungle, Kipling

Few are aware that Rudyard Kipling, the famed author of *The Jungle Book*, was once a landowner in the city of Vancouver. Kipling visited Vancouver three times in his life: once in the late 1889 when he was 23 and not overly well known, once in 1892 when his popularity was beginning to mount, and once in 1907, when he was far and away the most famous author in the world.

Kipling loved Vancouver and wrote about his 1889 visit in a travel memoir titled *From Sea to Sea and Other Sketches*. He described Vancouver's unused spittoons, honest, well-spoken men, absence of bustle and perfect harbour. Determined to buy land in the city, either upon which to settle down or to resell later once its value increased, he went into a real estate office and purchased three plots of land. Two were at the corner of Fraser and East Eleventh and the other was 20 acres of wilderness in North Vancouver.

Soon he came to realize that not everybody in Vancouver was quite as honest as he thought. Though Kipling paid tax on the North Vancouver property for a great many years, he later learned that the land already belonged to someone else; he had given his money to a swindler.

The two downtown properties were indeed his, but when he decided to resell them, he learned the city had developed in a different direction and the land had hardly appreciated. While he made a gross profit, the amount he had paid in property tax made it a net loss.

Thank goodness Kipling was such a great writer, because when it came to real estate, he was far less brilliant.

Pissed Off and Pissed On

Shannon Hoon, the lead singer of the popular American rock band Blind Melon, crossed all sorts of lines during a 1993 show at the Pacific Coliseum when he stripped off his clothes and performed his last three songs naked. He then urinated on a fan. Needless to say, he was drunk.

Immediately after the show, Vancouver police arrested Hoon and charged him with committing an indecent act and public nudity. He was sentenced to community service and ordered to pick up trash in Pigeon Park on East Hastings Street, one of the seediest spots along Vancouver's downtown east side. The park is notorious for its population of drug dealers and users, homeless people and the mentally ill. Hoon later wrote about the incident in a Blind Melon song called "Dump Truck."

Mars Makes Contact

Speaking of curious behaviour, in August 1924, the planet Mars was closer to Earth than at any point in the last 100 years, a mere 54 million kilometres away, 22 million closer than its regular distance. During this time, the Point Grey wireless station received unusual signals for nearly a month: four distinct groups of four dashes came in nearly every day, all of which were so powerful that they could not be "tuned out." The wireless operators said the signals were absolutely distinctive, not in any identifiable code and could not be attributed to any known communication instrument, leaking transformer or outside interference. The origin of the signals was never found, but on August 22, the *The Province* ran a story on the front page attributing the phenomenon to Martian contact.

ENTERTAINMENT TALES

Hollywood North

Often referred to as Hollywood North, Vancouver has been a major player in the filmmaking industry for over 100 years.

Vancouver was first used as a location in 1910, when the Edison Manufacturing Company shot *The Cowpuncher's Glove* and *The Ship's Husband* in the city, and since then, it's grown into the largest production centre for film and television in Canada, and the third largest in the world, just behind Los Angeles and New York City. In 2010 alone, almost 250 motion pictures were filmed in Vancouver, and a whopping $1.5 billion were spent producing them.

What's Vancouver got that other cities don't? A lot of things, actually. Until recently, the weak Canadian dollar made filming north of the 49th Parallel a savvy cost-cutting measure, and film crews love moving up from Los Angeles because the time zone doesn't change and the travel is nowhere near as intensive as a flight to New York. Furthermore, the Lower Mainland has so many unique buildings that it can double as nearly any American city and provides prime locales for almost every picture under the sun.

Speaking of the sun, the natural environment plays into it as well. Vancouver's mild weather allows for filming all year round, and the consistent cloud cover diffuses natural sunlight, allowing filmmakers to tweak the light in their films to their specifications. It also adds a certain level of eeriness at night. When *The X-Files* moved from Vancouver to Los Angeles after five seasons, it was impossible for the show's diehards to miss the spookiness sacrificed in the trip down south.

The Summer of Snow

In 1900, the Canadian Pacific Railway financed a promotional film that was intended to entice settlers into coming west to Vancouver. Unfortunately, it took over two years to make. Why? The filmmakers were forbidden from showing snow. This shouldn't have been a problem. While Vancouver's weather is notoriously unpredictable, snow in much rarer than in most other Canadian cities. However, the filmmakers couldn't get away from the snow. Not only did Vancouverites suffer two snowy winters in a row in those early days, but they also had to endure a snowy summer when on June 23, 1901, snow fell in South Vancouver.

A Record Number of Records

Some fabulously cool record collectors live in Vancouver, such as Rob Snopek, who rents two apartments in his Burnaby building —one to live in, and the other as appointment-only rare record shop called Music Madhouse. But the king of record collectors was Jack Cullen.

Cullen's late-night radio show *Owl Prowl* was a fixture of the Vancouver airwaves from the mid-1940s to the end of the century.

The man knew his music. He also owned quite a bit. There were more than 300,000 records, radio recordings and tapes in his collection, at one time considered the largest private collection in the world.

If you're a vinyl-head, this next part might make you gasp: just before his death in 2002, the entire collection was sold to someone for only $15,000, then disseminated via eBay. Good Lord. But don't lose respect for Cullen—the sale wasn't his doing. CKNW Radio purchased the record collection from Cullen in the early 1970s for $150,000, a much better figure.

Clearly, the radio station wasn't all that deserving of the collection, especially since they would later sell it for a tenth of what they paid for it, but lucky for us, Cullen didn't give CKNW everything. He kept a number of his private recordings, among which were some of the best bootleg records of all time. Cullen secretly recorded Frank Sinatra's 1957 concert at the Pacific National Exhibition. When Sinatra found out, he was furious.

On the flipside, Louis Armstrong was so impressed with the quality of Cullen's bootleg of one of his shows, he let Cullen release it as a limited-run LP.

But Cullen's best act as a bootlegger came when he successfully recorded The Beatles' infamous 27-minute 1964 concert at Empire Stadium. As stated earlier, the CBC recordings of that show have been destroyed but, despite attempts by Capitol records to do the same to Cullen's illegal album, a few copies are still floating around. If you have one, I'll trade you my house for it.

More Money, More Problems

Celebrity power-couple Goldie Hawn and Kurt Russell moved to Vancouver in late 2002, reportedly in support of son Wyatt's burgeoning hockey career. Wyatt, 15 at the time, was a goaltender for the Richmond Sockeyes.

Hawn and Russell's movements attracted tabloid attention during their shopping sprees and dinners at Vancouver's ritziest locales. After the pair purchased a $3-million mansion in upscale Shaughnessy, they allowed reporters from the *Vancouver Sun* to reveal its glorious interior and spectacular views in a full-colour spread in the paper. They were fixtures of the city for three years, after which time their son's minor hockey career ended and the couple sold their home and moved back to Los Angeles.

Plenty was written about them, but the best story to come out of their time in the city came when Goldie's Porsche was stolen from the couple's front yard—and they took three days to notice. "We are disgusting people," Russell said. "We should take a good look at ourselves."

ABOUT THE ILLUSTRATORS

Peter Tyler

Peter is a graduate of the Vancouver Film School's Visual Art and Design and Classical animation programs. Though his ultimate passion is in filmmaking, he is also intent on developing his draftsmanship and storytelling, with the aim of using those skills in future filmic misadventures.

Patrick Hénaff

Born in France, Patrick Hénaff is mostly self-taught. He is a versatile artist who has explored a variety of media under many different influences. He now uses primarily pen and ink to draw, and then processes the images on computer. He is particularly interested in the narrative power of pictures and tries to use them as a way to tell stories.

Roger Garcia

Roger Garcia is a self-taught artist with some formal training
who specializes in cartooning and illustration. He is an immigrant from El Salvador, and during the last few years, his work
has been primarily cartoons and editorial illustrations in pen and
ink. Recently, he has started painting once more. Focusing on
simplifying the human form, he uses a bright minimal palette
and as few elements as possible. His work can be seen in newspapers, magazines, promo material and on www.rogergarcia.ca.

Djordje Tordovic

Djordje is an artist/illustrator living in Toronto, Ontario. He first
moved to the city to go to York University to study fine arts. He got
a taste for illustrating while working as the illustrator for his college
paper, *Mondo Magazine*. He has since worked on various projects
and continues to perfect his craft. Aside from his artistic work,
Djordje devotes his time volunteering at the Print and Drawing
Centre at the Art Gallery of Ontario. When he is not doing that,
he is out trotting the globe.

Roly Wood

Roly has worked in Toronto as a freelance illustrator and was also employed in the graphic design department of a landscape architecture firm. In 2004, he wrote and illustrated a historical comic book set in Lang Pioneer Village near Peterborough, Ontario. To see more of Roly's work, visit www.rolywood.com.

Pat Bidwell

Pat has always had a passion for drawing and art. Initially self-taught, Pat completed art studies in visual communication in 1986. Over the years, he has worked both locally and internationally as an illustrator/product designer and graphic designer, collecting many awards for excellence along the way. When not at the drawing board, Pat pursues other interests solo and/or with his wife, Lisa.

ABOUT THE AUTHOR

Harrison Mooney

Born and raised in Vancouver, Harrison Mooney is a freelance writer, playwright, a songwriter and a musician. He is the editor of the *Vancouver Sun*'s Canucks hockey blog, *Pass it to Bulis*, and is also the associate editor of the Yahoo! Sports blog, *Puck Daddy*. Harrison was the editor of the Maple Stress Press *Canucks 2011 Annual* and was a contributor to the *Vancouver Sun/The Province* book, *A Thrilling Ride*. His work regularly appears in the *Vancouver Sun*.

Harrison says he eats peaches like it's their last day on the planet, he once sang the national anthem at a CIS basketball game and he shares a house with two gorgeous females—his wife and their cat.